THE NEAR-DEATH EXPERIENCE

CALVERT ROSZELL

THE NEAR-DEATH EXPERIENCE

IN THE LIGHT OF
SCIENTIFIC RESEARCH
AND THE SPIRITUAL SCIENCE
OF RUDOLF STEINER

With a Foreword by
George G. Ritchie, Jr., M.D.

THE ANTHROPOSOPHIC PRESS

The publisher gratefully acknowledges permission to quote from
Return to Tomorrow by George G. Ritchie © 1978 George G. Ritchie M.D.
Published by Chosen Books, Fleming H. Revell Company. Used by permission.

Text © 1992 Calvert Roszell
This edition © 1992 Anthroposophic Press

Published by Anthroposophic Press
RR4, Box 94 A-1, Hudson, NY 12534

Library of Congress Cataloging-in-Publication Data

Roszell, Calvert.
    The near-death experience: in the light of scientific research and the spiritual science
of Rudolf Steiner: with a foreword by George G. Ritchie, Jr. / Calvert Roszell.
      p. cm.
    Includes bibliographical references.
    ISBN 0-88010-360-4
    1. Anthroposophy. 2. Near-death experiences — Religious aspects. 3. Near-death
experiences — Case studies. 4. Ritchie, George G., 1923-   . 5. Steiner, Rudolf, 1861-
1925. I. Title.
  BP596.N43R67 1992
  133.9'01'3 — dc20
                          91-27842
                            CIP

10 9 8 7 6 5 4 3 2 1

Book Design by Jennie Reins

Printed in the United States of America

For Nancy Bradford Roszell,
who introduced me to George Ritchie.

WHERE DO WE FIND OURSELVES? IN A SERIES OF WHICH WE DO NOT KNOW THE EXTREMES, AND BELIEVE THAT IT HAS NONE. WE WAKE AND FIND OURSELVES ON A STAIR; THERE ARE STAIRS BELOW US, WHICH WE SEEM TO HAVE ASCENDED; THERE ARE STAIRS ABOVE US, MANY A ONE, WHICH GO UPWARD AND OUT OF SIGHT. BUT THE GENIUS WHICH ACCORDING TO THE OLD BELIEF STANDS AT THE DOOR BY WHICH WE ENTER, AND GIVES US THE LETHE TO DRINK, THAT WE MAY TELL NO TALES, MIXED THE CUP TOO STRONGLY, AND WE CANNOT SHAKE OFF THE LETHARGY NOW AT NOONDAY. SLEEP LINGERS ALL OUR LIFETIME ABOUT OUR EYES, AS NIGHT HOVERS ALL DAY IN THE BOUGHS OF THE FIR-TREE.

— *Ralph Waldo Emerson*

CONTENTS

FOREWORD

Calvert Theodore Roszell, better known to his friends as Ted, came into my life through a letter he wrote more than two years ago after having read my book, thanking me for sharing my near-death experience and expressing his sincere interest in it. Over the next two years we exchanged many letters. At my invitation, he flew down for a fishing trip we made together. Getting to know each other personally has created a warm place in my heart.

Though I have spent most of my adult life working with young people, I have never met one who was as intensely interested in coming to understand what happens to us after we die. Through his letters and through getting to know him in person, I have come to realize that this is due to Ted's intense interest in the spiritual destiny of man.

Researchers have found that the people who are most successful in life have chosen their vocation or profession early in life. Calvert Roszell is no exception; he showed a profound interest in the German language when he heard it for the first time at the age of seven, leading him eventually to learn the language at college and earn scholarships to Germany.

His studies in German led him to the works of Rudolf Steiner, who had the same interest that Calvert has had. The life and work of Steiner greatly intensified Calvert's interest both in the spiritual side of the human being and also in the state of the individual in life after death. It was only natural that, as a writer and a philosopher, Calvert should also become interested in near-death experiences and write this book. The book is excellent and reflects considerable research and study as well as deep spiritual insight.

To me, however, the most significant results in this young man's life are the love, gentleness, compassion and interest he has developed for his fellow human beings. In demonstrating these qualities in his own life, he shows that he has already come to personally know Christ and is carrying out His commandment to love others as he has been loved. He has learned to do this without having to undergo a near-death experience himself in order to have his life changed.

I consider it a privilege to recommend this book to anyone who wishes to gain a better understanding of some of the things that may happen to us as we pass through death and the gateways it opens to us.

Respectfully,
George G. Ritchie, Jr., M.D.

PREFACE

In this book we will look at the mystery of life from the perspective of near-death experiences. Much has been said and written about the phenomenon of near-death experiences since the appearance of Dr. Raymond Moody's book *Life After Life* in 1975, but the extent to which scientific research — such as the work of Dr. Michael Sabom, a noted cardiologist and professor of medicine at Emory University — can show that these are actually out-of-body or spiritual experiences has largely been ignored. Similarly, the remarkable parallels, even in the smallest details, between the near-death account of Dr. George G. Ritchie, a respected psychiatrist from Virginia, and the spiritual vision of Rudolf Steiner (1861-1925), the prolific Austrian philosopher, educator, and writer, have also not received the attention they deserve. It was George Ritchie's account of his near-death experience that led Raymond Moody to his insightful study, which in turn has inaugurated widespread contemporary interest in this phenomenon.

George Ritchie is a rugged, darkly tanned, handsome outdoorsman of Scottish descent; he speaks directly and forcefully with a gentle Virginian accent. He strikes one as a man who is completely at peace with himself and the world, and he has a rare talent for making everyone completely at ease in his company. The variety and depth of his life have made him a fine storyteller; he is an excellent fisherman and generous with the day's catch. Recently retired from his private practice, he lives at the oceanside with his wife and companion Marguerite Shell Ritchie, who shares his warmth and steadiness. Ritchie continues to give talks on subjects ranging from cognitive therapy in psychiatry to the mystery of his near-death experience as an army recruit in the winter of 1943.

After considering the scientific principles applicable to near-death experiences as well as their inherent limitations, we will compare George Ritchie's account of his experience with Rudolf Steiner's description of the spiritual realm. The clarity of both these accounts illustrates the close and inextricable relationship between our direct experience and cognition and the world around us. Regardless of the conclusions about near-death experiences that readers may ultimately arrive at — may this essay be a source of new perspectives and food for thought.

ACKNOWLEDGMENTS

The author owes a debt of thanks to Sabine H. Seiler and Judith Sweningsen for their acumen and care in the editing of the manuscript. Special thanks also to my wife, Hanna Elisabeth Reincke, to Dr. Frederick Amrine, Professor of German language and literature at the University of Michigan, as well as to Bruce and Ruth Nilsson, and to Maria Gracanin for encouragement and support in the writing and lecturing stages of this monograph.

PART ONE

THE RIDDLE OF CONSCIOUSNESS

THE PRESENT STATE OF RESEARCH INTO NEAR-DEATH EXPERIENCES

NEAR-DEATH EXPERIENCES (NDE) are among the most thought-provoking mysteries of human life, and fully understanding them will have far-reaching consequences. Are these experiences the hallucinations of a brain depleted of oxygen, or are they a reconnaissance into spiritual worlds?

To pursue these questions is to come face to face with the mind-body problem and that of the origin of consciousness. Is the mind merely a chimera of neurophysiology, nothing but a figment of the imagination? Or are our brain and senses the instruments of our consciousness? Evidence for the resolution of this impasse comes from medicine and physiology as well as from our ephemeral but direct psychological and intuitive perceptions. How are these two modes of knowledge related? Are they in conflict or do they complement each other?

To begin with, let us look at the facts and how they are described. Apparently, near-death experiences have always been a part of human existence; they are described, for example, in the Tibetan and the Egyptian Books of the Dead. Later, Plato narrates such an experience in clear detail in book 10 of *The Republic*, and it will serve us well to take this as our starting point.

Plato tells the story of Er, a soldier given up for dead on the battlefield, who awakens on the funeral pyre from a most remarkable voyage. Er then relates that his soul rose out of his body and joined a company of others in a strange place where two openings in the earth met two openings into the heavens. A group of judges seated there commanded the just to ascend to heaven through the portal at the right. The unjust were compelled to pass into the subterranean regions through the portal at the left. Then follow vivid descriptions of the sufferings and punishments of these souls — the results of their wickedness in past lives and of their constant fear of falling into the abyss and becoming lost forever. Er also accompanied the other souls into the upper world, where a festival on a meadow was in progress. The party came to a place where heaven and earth were made translucent with an effulgent light, brighter and purer than any of nature's rainbows. Here, others in the company were called to draw lots to meet a mysterious genius or guide, who would lead them into their new lives. Then these souls drank from the cup of forgetfulness. In the shapes of stars, these souls appeared to hop away, one this way, the next another, to begin another turn of the wheel of the life of mortals. Er had been held back at the border of the river Lethe, and he awakened on the pyre.

Remarkable narratives similar to Er's have become widely known in the past few decades. This is due in no small measure to the advances in the technology of resuscitation, which are now bringing so many people back from near-death, and to the wide international circulation of literature on the subject, particularly since 1975 when Raymond Moody's book *Life after Life* first appeared.

Moody's book is the result of one of the most significant meetings of his life, the beginning of his friendship with George G. Ritchie, Jr. In 1965, Moody was an undergraduate majoring in philosophy at the University of Virginia where Dr. Ritchie was on the psychiatry faculty at the School of Medicine. Ritchie's story of a vivid journey into another world after having been pronounced dead in a boot camp hospital presented Moody with a mystery he would wrestle with for many years to come.

In 1969, Moody completed his doctorate in philosophy and joined the faculty at a university in eastern North Carolina. Following a discussion of Plato's idea of immortality in *Phaedo*, one of Moody's students came to see him in his office. After a brush with death in the operating room, the student's grandmother had shared an experience of apparent immortality with her grandson. The student told Moody about his grandmother's story. The details vividly reminded Moody of his meeting with George Ritchie and kindled a strong desire in him to understand what lay behind such experiences.

He began his inquiry and changed his career, entering medical school in 1972. In his studies, he began to collect accounts of close encounters with death and found them all remarkably similar to Ritchie's. Moody compiled 150 of these accounts of persons who had shared their stories with him in his book.[1]

According to Moody, both the details and the sequence of events in the narratives of persons who survive close encounters with death tend to coincide. The experience may begin with a loud buzzing, ringing, or musical sound, suddenly followed by an impression of flying through a dark tunnel. The phenomenon called autoscopy may follow; typically, it entails the shock of apparently standing or floating next to oneself while doctors or medics furiously attempt to resuscitate the body. Once the individual has become somewhat used to this new state of affairs, he or she notices what appears to be a new body with completely unfamiliar properties. Soon after that, deceased relatives or friends may appear to draw near, and at some point an indescribably bright light or being of light may perhaps also approach. This figure may guide the individual through a panoramic recall of everything he or she has experienced in life.

If the experience continues, the near-dead person may enter a state of transcendent, life-transforming peace and may eventually reach a kind of border he or she is not allowed to cross. Instead, the person seems to be suddenly pulled back into his or her earthly body with a tug. Generally, this experience becomes a catalyst for a tumultuous reorganization of the individual's fundamental values and insights in the days and weeks that follow.

Moody was aware that the scientific value of his anecdotal fieldwork was limited and left much work for others. Nevertheless, he knew that his efforts led people to pay attention and take seriously these remarkably consistent accounts of otherworldly experiences. Many neurologists, psychologists, and psychiatrists became fascinated with the riddle of near-death experiences, and much has been learned in recent years about the circumstances surrounding them.[2] Moody then convened a group including John Audette, Kenneth Ring, Bruce Greyson, Michael Sabom,

---

1. Raymond Moody, *Life After Life* (Atlanta: Mockingbird, 1975).

and many other interested researchers who had written to him after his book appeared, and in November 1977 a research foundation for the study of near-death experiences was formed.[1]

An important study by Kenneth Ring, a professor of psychology at the University of Connecticut, appeared in 1980 and, on the whole, it seemed to confirm the basic elements of Moody's characterization of near-death experiences.[2] However, Ring's informants generally did not report the buzzing or ringing sounds or clear impressions of a second body, and images of open spaces often replaced the tunnel image.[3] Further investigations were clearly called for, especially since the research team had not been rigorous in selecting unbiased reports. They had to resort to newspaper advertisements to obtain reports, and occasionally they also employed biased interviewing practices, such as asking the leading question of whether the near-death survivor had "at any time experienced a light, glow, or illumination?"[4] Nevertheless, later studies revealed that these deficiencies were not significant.

Michael B. Sabom, professor of medicine at Emory University and cardiologist at the Atlanta VA Medical Center, was skeptical but interested enough to undertake the first carefully controlled medical study of NDEs.[5] For this study, which was published in 1982, he and his collaborator, Sarah Kreutziger, routinely interviewed patients in the intensive care and dialysis units of two Florida hospitals.[6]

2. Current comprehensive bibliographies on NDE research can be found in Terry K. Basforth, *The Near Death Experience: An Annotated Bibliography* (New York: Garland Publishing, 1990), in Carol Zaleski, *Otherworld Journeys* (New York: Oxford University Press, 1987), pp. 257-266, as well as in the 1990 study of near-death experiences in children by Melvin Morse, *Closer To The Light* (New York: Villard Books, 1990).

1. Association for the Scientific Study of Near-Death Phenomena, renamed the International Association for Near-Death Studies (IANDS), c/o Department of Psychiatry, University of Connecticut Health Center, Farmington, CT 06032. Bruce Greyson, M.D., is currently Director of Research.

2. Kenneth Ring, *Life at Death: A Scientific Investigation* (New York: Coward, McCann & Geoghegan, 1980).

3. Carol Zaleski, *Otherworld Journeys* (New York: Oxford University Press, 1987), p. 106.

4. Zaleski, pp. 105, 106.

5. Michael B. Sabom, *Recollections of Death* (New York: Simon & Schuster, 1982). See also interview by Claudia Willis "A Doctor Studies Patients' Recollections of Dying," in *Time*, February 8, 1982, p. 79.

6. Zaleski, p. 109. Dr. Kenneth Ring's study, entitled *Life at Death* (1980), ran concurrently with Dr. Sabom's. However, Ring's study relied, as did Moody's, on advertised or solicited data (see Zaleski, p.105). The Sabom study did not, and it is therefore the basis of the research report presented here.

Sabom found, somewhat to his surprise, that his study corroborated Moody's basic findings again and again. Sabom's subjects often confirmed the details of Ring's characterizations in the instances where the latter diverged from Moody's. Occasionally, the language Sabom's subjects used to describe their experiences was reminiscent of that Moody had reported in his book. For example, the patients Sabom interviewed often described a feeling of moving through a void rather than through a tunnel, but some also likened the experience to that of traveling down a kind of "corridor."[1]

On the basis of his research, Sabom concluded that there is presently no physiological explanation that can account for near-death experiences. He found that the data he had collected indicates, but does not conclusively prove, that NDEs are body-free states of consciousness. He noted many consistent physical differences between NDEs and other, seemingly similar states as well as the fact that NDEs can occur in the absence of any physical or mental pathological condition. Most surprisingly, he also found numerous instances of patients having accurately observed their surroundings during their near-death experiences even though they would not have been able to make such observations under ordinary waking conditions. Some reported only details of the physical environment at the site of an accident or the hospital; others reported a chain of events leading to a transcendental world.

In the wake of Sabom's study, research on near-death experiences has continued in many directions, but scientific interpretation of the results is by no means uniform. Having brought all the relevant fields of natural science to bear on the question, we still do not have the kind of blueprint or formula we get for the way a watch works or a planetary orbit runs. Thus, we are easily swayed by whatever opinions we hear most frequently on this subject. We may deceive ourselves that we are arriving at a considered judgment even though we really have done nothing more than recite newspaper clippings and conversations.

The opinions and judgments arrived at in this way will most certainly have to be revised, and we have to ask ourselves whether we are able to

---

1. Sabom, p. 42.

actively take part in this process of change. From a certain perspective, it may seem a matter of supreme indifference whether we are in fact actively engaged in the inquiry of knowledge and whether we are willing to be changed by the results of our inquiry. However, what we know, or think we know, is the foundation of our attitudes, expectations, and values; it informs our intentions and thus our actions. Clearly, then, our answer to the fundamental question of the nature of the human soul shapes what we value and strive for—whether we are aware of this or not. Our answer will also define how far we can go in our continuous remaking of nature and the world according to our will and purposes. Our attitudes concerning our soul in life and death are thus inextricably linked to our responsibility for the earth.

The Temporal Lobe Seizure Hypothesis

To avoid forming a superficial view of the nature of near-death experiences, let us first consider some of the settings in which the elements of these experiences occur. Our approach to a key element begins with a remarkable scientific discovery of the twentieth century. In 1933, the Canadian neurosurgeon Wilder Penfield was treating patients suffering from epileptic seizures. One day, he was mapping the cortex of a patient's brain with a lightly charged electrode to avoid damaging the brain later during surgery. Since the brain is not very sensitive to pain, he used only a mild local anesthetic, and his patient was conscious.[1]

Penfield was astonished when, at the touch of the electrode to the exposed cortex, the patient found herself in her kitchen and heard her little boy playing outside as well as the sound of traffic. Penfield began to research this phenomenon and found that when he touched certain areas of the brain with the electrode, his subjects relived long forgotten events so vividly that they even felt the forgotten moods and emotions accompanying those events.

Thus, Penfield discovered that everything that happens to us may be indelibly inscribed in the recesses of our memories. In light of this insight, it is interesting that people often report having seen their whole lives pass

---

1. Wilder Penfield, *The Mystery of the Mind* (Princeton: Princeton University Press, 1975).

vividly before their eyes during their near-death experiences. Did Penfield's discovery offer an explanation for this? A number of neurologists have speculated along these lines and have concluded that NDEs involve the same neurophysiological activity that occurred in Penfield's patients.

However, Sabom found that this tack leads to untenable generalizations. According to his research, for example, the senses of smell and taste are not stimulated during NDEs, but they often are in epileptic seizures. Sabom also found that the forced thinking characteristic of the seizures ("the crowding of random thoughts and ideas into the mind of the patient in an automatic and obtrusive way") is conspicuously absent in NDEs.[1] Nevertheless, the similarities between the revival of memory under Penfield's electrode and the panoramic review during NDEs are striking although they remain unexplained. Further research was indicated, and important new applications of Penfield's work have been discovered since Sabom's study was published.

Melvin Morse, a pediatrician who directed a research team that carefully examined Penfield's work, found case histories in a forty-year-old textbook by Penfield that shed further light on the question.[2] Electrical stimulation of an area of the temporal lobe just above the right ear had caused some of Penfield's patients to report that they seemed to be leaving their bodies. Stimulation of nearby surrounding areas led to reports of visions of deceased relatives and friends or of God as well as to descriptions of majestic music in addition to the panoramic life review. Morse and his team published a paper on their study in 1986,[3] and a group of neurologists in Chile responded that their own independent research confirmed that neuronal activity of the Sylvian fissure appears to be the cause of the NDE phenomenon.

While this may seem to be the end of the mystery of near-death experiences, it is actually only the beginning of the mystery of consciousness. In his most recent study of near-death experiences in children, Morse concludes that the activity at the Sylvian fissure does not fully explain

---

1. Sabom, p.174.
2. Wilder Penfield and Theodore Rasmussen, *The Cerebral Cortex of Man* (New York: Macmillan, 1950).
3. M. Morse, P. Castillo, D. Venecia, et al. "Childhood Near-Death Experiences," *American Journal of Diseases of Children* 140 (1986):1110-1113.

NDEs but only deepens the mystery of the phenomenon.[1] He cites the part of Sabom's study indicating that the out-of-body reports of cardiac patients near death included detailed and accurate descriptions of the resuscitation procedures, at least some of which could not have been witnessed from the vantage point of the body even if the patients had been conscious. Morse finds that Sabom's report is strong evidence that the mind or soul in fact separates from the body under such conditions. We will return to the implications of this part of Sabom's study for the mind-body problem, but only after trying to answer the lesser question of whether the different elements of near-death experiences, such as the life review or visions of deceased relatives, occur only under life-threatening circumstances.

We have already seen that Penfield's work shows that the panoramic review takes place not only near death but also at the touch of a mildly charged electrode. We will see that any number of physical conditions, and even emotional or psychological ones, may lead to this experience. Each of these various conditions gives rise to one or more of the elements common to near-death experiences.

Hypoxia

Ernst A. Rodin, a neurologist who had undergone a near-death experience himself, which he described as "one of the most intense and happiest moments of [my] life," concluded that the experience was nevertheless most likely nothing more than the hallucination of a brain starved for oxygen, and he published a research paper on his experience.[2] Rodin characterizes a reduced supply of oxygen, or hypoxia, as the "final common pathway" of death. For example, if the heart stops beating for whatever reason, the circulation also ceases; there is no pulse or blood pressure. The blood can no longer carry oxygen to nourish the organs essential to life. These deteriorate rapidly, and death ensues. For example, a person may have a drowning accident and not be able to breathe for three minutes. This results in irreversible brain damage, and in a few

---

1. Melvin Morse, *Closer To The Light* (New York: Villard Books, 1990) pp. 103, 104.
2. Ernst Rodin, "The Reality of Death Experiences: A Personal Perspective," *Journal of Nervous and Mental Disease* 168 (May 1980):259-263.

minutes more, none of the life-sustaining organs can be saved. Again, death is the end result.

However, hypoxia is not only the final pathway of death. It may also trigger seizure activity deep within the brain, in the limbic system, the site associated with the faculties of memory, mood, and emotion.[1] And the "aura" or premonitions that precede these seizures may include a spontaneous, unbidden revival of memory. Since hypoxia accompanies death and may also cause an unusual revival of memory, some neurologists, including Rodin, conclude that agitation of the limbic system is the physiological basis for near-death experiences.

Stanislav Grof, former chief of psychiatric research at the Maryland Psychiatric Research Center, assistant professor of psychiatry at Johns Hopkins University, and author of several books on the effects of hallucinogenic drugs, has come to similar conclusions.[2] He points out that hypoxia may be a particularly relevant context for visions of many kinds, because various religious practices induce both visionary experiences and hypoxia. For example, in Indian Yoga techniques, alternating periods of hyperventilation and prolonged retention of the breath may lead to visions as well as to hypoxia. Other similar practices, such as obstruction of the larynx by turning back the tongue, have the same effect. Near suffocation under water also appears to have been a means of inducing such altered states in earlier cultures. In fact, the earliest form of baptism seems to have involved holding neophytes under water until the point of near drowning, a practice that caused profound near-death and rebirth experiences. (Interestingly enough, the cisterns at Qumran may well have served this function in the practices of the Essenes, with whom many scholars believe that John the Baptist had contact.) Visionary experiences have also been sought through smoke inhalation; the concomitant physiology is again hypoxia.

It seems reasonable to hypothesize with Rodin and Grof that the same course of events also obtains in near-death experiences. However, in his

---

1. See, for example, Zaleski, p. 166. For a precise and highly readable discussion of the role of the limbic system in mental functions, see chapter 3 of Carl Sagan's *The Dragons of Eden* (New York: Random House, 1977).
2. Stanislav Grof and Joan Halifax, *The Human Encounter With Death* (New York: Dutton, 1977), p. 184.

research Sabom came to the conclusion that hypoxia is an inadequate explanation for NDEs because the latter may occur in the absence of the former. Sabom presents the example of a patient under his own care whose blood oxygen and carbon dioxide levels had been measured at the time of his cardiac arrest and the accompanying near-death experience. Indeed, the events must have taken place simultaneously because the patient's report of the near-death experience includes a description of the blood oxygen test. In fact, cardiopulmonary resuscitation had increased the patient's blood oxygen to a level above normal.[1] Sabom concedes that this one instance does probably not constitute decisive evidence. Yet, it should be pointed out that regardless of the oxygen level in the femoral artery, an insufficiency of blood circulation (ischemia) could have led to very different conditions at the critical sites in the brain during the resuscitation and the near-death experience.

In addition, Sabom found that careful attention to the phenomenology of the NDE uncovers differences too significant to allow for broad generalizations equating the hypoxic and the near-death states. Hypoxia is consistently associated with a progressive muddling and confusion of cognitive abilities, mental laziness, heightened irritability, difficulty in concentrating, slowness in reasoning, and difficulty in remembering — characteristics that contrast sharply with the clarity of thinking and awareness consistently apparent during near-death experiences and with the remarkable precision and breadth of detail in which they tend to be remembered.[2]

Hypercarbia

Some authorities suggest that elevated levels of carbon dioxide in the brain may be the cause of near-death experiences. The circulation of the blood ordinarily removes carbon dioxide waste from the tissues while supplying them with oxygen, but this process may slow or cease at the approach of death. What is the effect of such an event on consciousness?

In the 1950s, L. J. Meduna, a University of Illinois psychiatrist, carried out a study that answers this question. His subjects breathed a mixture of

---

1. Sabom, p. 178. The actual values were $pO_2 = 138$, $pCO_2 = 28$, $pH = 7.46$.
2. Ibid, p. 176.

30% oxygen and 70% carbon dioxide (air normally contains 21% oxygen and 0% carbon dioxide).[1] They typically experienced bright light, bodily detachment, revival of past memories as well as what they described as telepathic communication with a religious presence and feelings of cosmic importance and ecstasy. Melvin Morse — the Seattle pediatrician who showed that Penfield had described NDE phenomenology by electrically stimulating the Sylvian fissure of his patients' right temporal lobe — believes the Meduna mixture's carbon dioxide in fact triggers near-death experiences.

However, Sabom concludes that hypercarbia is no more an explanation of near-death experiences than hypoxia. A more sensitive description of the hypercarbic phenomenology reveals features that are consistently absent in near-death experiences, such as the perception of brightly colored geometric figures or patterns (like stained glass windows), animation of fantasized objects (such as musical notes floating by), polyopic vision, and frightening sensations of shapeless and objectless horror. It is particularly interesting that Meduna frequently found compulsions to solve mathematical puzzles in his subjects — a feature very similar to the forced thinking that characterizes temporal lobe seizures but is not typical of near-death experiences.

Finally, Sabom reports having tested the carbon dioxide as well as the oxygen level in the bloodstream of the cardiac patient whose report of his near-death experience included a description of the femoral artery blood test.[2] The subject was not suffering from hypercarbia.

Hallucinogenic Drugs

Sabom does note, however, that some of his subjects were under the influence of morphine or some other drug at the time of their NDEs, and some authorities suggest that these drugs may cause the NDEs. In experiments with cannabis for example, Ronald K. Siegel, psychopharmacologist at UCLA School of Medicine, found that his subjects often reported experiencing a bright light and tunnel perspective, revival of childhood

---

1. L. J. Meduna, "The Effect of Carbon Dioxide upon the Functions of the Brain," *Carbon Dioxide Therapy* (Springfield, IL: Thomas, 1950), pp. 23, 24, 28.
2. Sabom, p. 178.

memories, a vision of the physical body from above, and a sense of heightened reality.[1]

However, it should be noted that this hallucinogenic phenomenology is in dispute; on the basis of his emergency room experience, Morse asserts that narcotics do not cause the experiences of bright light or tunnel perspective reported by Siegel and adds that visions of spirits, heaven, and God are also absent.[2] Nevertheless, we have to keep in mind that Morse's objections are anecdotal and do not form a part of his study; Siegel's work, on the other hand, is a documented scientific investigation. A more fundamental objection against using the physiology of drug-induced hallucinations to explain near-death experiences is the fact that perception of the environment is distorted under the influence of drugs but not in near-death experiences. Sabom cites the example of a nearby watch that becomes a ticking bomb in the mind of the drugged person. In reporting near-death experiences, however, people describe nearby objects and events very accurately.[3] Sabom also notes the subtle and pervasive sense of identity loss and detachment reported by subjects under the influence of hallucinogens, a certain "not me" quality or spectator role. Interestingly, persons surviving near-death experiences speak of awakening to an even clearer and more substantial sense of self than they previously had in ordinary consciousness.[4]

The Search for a Common Physiological Basis for NDEs

How significant are the above-mentioned differences between the various physically induced hallucinations and near-death experiences? Is there some common basis underlying the constellation of drug, seizure, hypoxic, and hypercarbic states?

Stanislav Grof refers to "laboratory evidence that LSD may interfere with the transfer of oxygen on the enzymatic level," that is, at the level of the cells utilizing oxygen, which may point to a close relationship

---

1. "Hallucinations," Scientific American, October, 1977, pp. 132-140.
2. Morse, p. 184.
3. Sabom, pp. 104, 112, 115.
4. Ibid., p. 169.

between hypoxia and psychotropic drug hallucinations.[1] According to Siegel, pharmacological research "points to underlying mechanisms in the central nervous system as the source of a universal phenomenology of hallucinations"; many of the subjects in his own study perceived identical complex images under the influence of hallucinogenic drug. On the basis of the sharply defined perceptions, such as geometric shapes, reported commonly by his hypercarbic subjects, Meduna similarly concluded that such uniformly altered perceptions must have to do with "some underlying physiological function of some brain structures" regardless of personal differences among the subjects.

However, their research does not indicate just what such an underlying mechanism could be. It does probably not involve a lack of oxygen since Meduna's carbon dioxide mixture — which actually increased the blood oxygen level in test subjects — caused hallucinations so closely related to those induced by LSD that, by extrapolation, researchers could reliably predict what would happen to a given subject under the influence of LSD. Siegel's and Grof's observations do not appear to lead to any fundamental principles either.

Another relevant neurophysiological principle is that a vast possible range of neuronal firings is constantly modulated or suppressed in the healthy organism while useful firings are released only selectively. Through damage to the central nervous system in the process of death or related trauma, the organism might not be able to suppress mass random firings and the resulting electrical storms and hallucinations deep within the brain. At this point we can begin to appreciate the significance of the missing puzzle piece that Morse and Penfield found: heightened electrical activity in the right temporal lobe along the Sylvian fissure may accompany the NDE phenomena of autoscopy, vision of spirits, celestial music, and panoramic review.

And yet here, too, there does not seem to be a direct correlation between near-death experiences and specific physiological processes. NDE phenomena also frequently occur under circumstances of perfect health, due merely to momentary fear of imminent physical injury.

---

1. Grof and Halifax, p. 184.

The Biochemistry of Emotions

After having become familiar with the various physiological explanations, such as seizure activity, hypoxia, hypercarbia, and hallucinogenic drugs, we may be surprised to learn that mere fear of severe injury can actually lead to a near-death experience. Yet Moody coined the term to include just such instances, which Russell Noyes, professor of psychiatry, and Roy Kletti, clinical psychologist (both at the University of Iowa), agree belong to the profile of near-death experiences.

Noyes and Kletti were fascinated by the untranslated account of Albert Heim, a Zürich professor of geology who during an Alpine climbing trip in 1871 dropped seventy feet in a free fall and lived to tell about it. In the course of their research, Noyes and Kletti found that under such conditions many people experience vivid, racing thoughts, detachment from the body and surroundings, feelings of unreality, lack of emotion, an expanded sense of time, freedom from pain, calm, objectivity, narrowed focus of attention, and sharper vision and/or hearing. This phase is sometimes followed by life-review elements and then in some cases by a stage of transcendent or mystical experience.[1]

The experiences we are talking about here occur in healthy individuals and take only a few seconds. Noyes and Kletti applied a Freudian model to the facts and speculated that people entertain a fantasy of survival from the point of view of a disinterested spectator under these conditions as part of a depersonalization syndrome. However, Noyes and Kletti's research only makes NDEs all the more puzzling since they can apparently occur under particular mental and emotional conditions as well as under specific physical conditions.

Consequently, scientists tried to find the common denominator of these physical and mental-emotional conditions. The neuropsychologist Daniel Carr of the Massachusetts General Hospital proposed a comprehensive explanation. Carr emphasized that NDE subjects are rarely the epileptic patients of Penfield, but they are certainly subject to the universal neurochemistry of stress. He looked in this direction for an explanation of the

---

1. Noyes and Kletti concluded that these changes reflect the biological purpose of enhancing the efficiency of survival efforts. See Zaleski, p. 173.

NDE phenomena. Carr pointed out that endogenous opioid peptides, such as endorphins and enkephalins (morphinelike chemicals secreted by certain brain cells during extreme stress), accompany cerebral hypoxia in cases of near-death, and they are also secreted in response to a broad variety of injuries to the body, including infection, trauma, severe psychological distress, and even to some degree mere vigorous exercise.[1] It would appear to follow that endorphins could provide an explanation for near-death experiences. The advantage of Carr's hypothesis is that it applies to situations of physical injury as well as to those of a mere threat of imminent harm.

Sabom, however, found that the characteristic effect of the proposed substance does not match the characteristic profile of near-death experiences.[2] Sabom cites a study on B-endorphin in which subjects reported perceptions of venipuncture (the sting of a needle) and light touch; people surviving near-death experiences, on the other hand, report a total absence of pain and discomfort during the experience and a sudden return of pain as soon as their near-death experience is over. In contrast, the effect of endorphins increases and dissipates only gradually. Thus, if a massive release of B-endorphins occurred in NDEs, the anesthetic effect would persist longer than the few seconds or minutes a typical near-death experience lasts. In addition, release of B-endorphins causes somnolence and sleep, not the hyperalertness and clarity of vision and thinking consistently reported in NDEs. Finally, the sense of unreality engendered by the endorphin release distinguishes it from the experience of the near-death state. However, Sabom is unable to explain why the remarkable tableau of memories is evoked under both of these conditions. It is certainly conceivable that this strangely unique common feature is more significant than the differences between the other attendant features.

The Limits of Measure: The Natural Sciences and Epistemology

The physiological observations from the work of Penfield and Morse may indicate that one or perhaps an entire scale of conditions, ranging

---

1. Zaleski, p.166.
2. Sabom, pp.171-173.

from fear to intoxication, might stimulate the Sylvian fissure and lead to near-death experiences. If that is true, the question can be posed more narrowly yet: Do near-death experiences result from electrical activity in a particular site of the brain, or do they result from the loss of normal function of that brain part? This is the point of departure Morse chose for his work. He achieves what Carr had hoped to attain, namely, the identification of a plausible biochemical condition that could trigger near-death experiences.

At this juncture it is necessary to inquire into the ramifications of a potential discovery that near-death experiences in fact occur only when the neurons of the Sylvian fissure are overstimulated or otherwise acting contrary to their ordinary healthy function. Such a finding would still not answer whether such an electrochemical disarrangement is the cause of the near-death vision itself or only of the release of the soul from its bodily instrument and from the concomitant ordinary state of awareness.

We cannot expect any laboratory experiment to answer that question, anymore than we can expect consciousness itself to appear as an object of the physical senses. Our finest instruments, both our bodily senses and our scientific apparatus, remain blind and deaf to what distinguishes near-death experiences from an array of apparently related, pathological states caused by epilepsy, hallucinogens, or the touch of an electrode. No instrument can register even the faintest trace of the loss of the healthy, ordinary self-awareness. None can indicate the presence of the thinking will. This distinguishes the near-death state from the pathological conditions, and it is also the measureless, invisible substance of all our thoughts, including our scientific insights and all that we in essence are.

Through the natural sciences we can learn to know the diverse manifestations of the intelligence of nature, but in this way we still never meet that intelligence itself face to face. "Unbidden and without warning she sweeps us away in the round of her dance," wrote Goethe of nature. "We live within her and are strangers to her. She speaks perpetually with us and does not betray her secret."[1] Goethe's words are a strikingly accurate portrayal of the epistemological value of the natural sciences. His statement

---

1. Johann Wolfgang von Goethe, *Scientific Studies*, edited and translated by Douglas Miller (New York: Suhrkamp, 1988), p. 3.

is neither trivial nor mere lip service; he loved the natural sciences and made positive contributions to their development.

The Insufficiency of Other Explanations of Near-Death Experiences

A number of other explanations for near-death experiences have been advanced and discarded in Sabom's study. These include the psychiatric model of autoscopic hallucination, subconscious fabrication, and prior expectations. In psychiatric cases of autoscopic hallucinations, subjects do not relate that they seem to leave the body and view it from above; instead, they report seeing a shadowy double of the physical body, often only from the shoulders up. These experiences involve direct interaction between the body and the projected double — the image appears to mimic the subject's gestures — and they are perceived as unreal and commonly evoke only negative emotions.[1] This phenomenon is clearly different from the autoscopy associated with near-death experiences; however, it is characteristic of epilepsy, temporal lobe dysfunction, brain trauma, alcoholism, and schizophrenia, a fact that further underscores the uniqueness of near-death experiences. The notion of prior expectations refers to the familiar phenomenon of people's hallucinations fulfilling their deepest desires and expectations; for example, the old and tired seek rest and find the fulfillment of that wish in hallucinations of meadows and golden streets. However, in his study, Sabom found little precedent in the subjects' imaginations for the remarkable details they typically reported about their near-death experiences.[2] Sabom also observed that near-death experiences differ markedly from dreams in the strong sense of reality that accompanies the former according to his subjects' reports.[3]

Accurate Reconnaissance of Physical Surroundings

The fact that sedated or comatose patients undergoing a near-death experience afterwards often report exact details of their surroundings is both baffling and telling. Such a state of affairs contradicts the physiological and

---

1. Sabom, p. 165.
2. Ibid., pp. 166-68.
3. Ibid., p. 166.

psychiatric explanations advanced above and brings us face to face with the mind-body problem. Melvin Morse finds this a compelling basis for viewing the role of the Sylvian fissure as merely intermediary instead of as completely explanatory. Sabom noted in his study that these patients actually describe things they could not have seen even if they had been awake. The patient described above, whose blood test at the time of his cardiac arrest appears to negate the hypoxia and hypercarbia explanations in his case, correctly described the patterns the needles made in the dials of a defibrillator.[1] Another patient identified three family members standing outside in a corridor although he was at no point in a position to have seen them.[2] Raymond Moody documented similar accounts; for example, he writes about a brother and sister who were both near death in different wings of the same hospital. The brother had an autoscopic near-death experience from one corner of his room when his sister appeared at his side. She seemed to draw away, saying, "You can't go with me because it's not your time." The brother survived and reported that his sister had just died — which was true.[3]

Dreaming during hypnogogic sleep, that is, when falling asleep, is obviously not a possible explanation since we see nothing around us in sleep. There remains the question of semiconscious perception since the sense of hearing functions close to the limits of unconsciousness and death. Is language in the environment being overheard and then translated into mental images? Apparently not, Michael Sabom points out, because under hypnotic regression it has been shown that language heard in semiconsciousness is not translated into visual images. Moreover, pain is still felt in the semiconscious state, but, as we have noted, it is completely absent during near-death experiences. Some people who have survived near-death experiences were even able to distinguish between overheard conversations and the ensuing tableau they saw during their experience.[4] The efforts of the intellect to understand the phenomenon of near-death experiences seem to end in speculations on coincidences.

---

1. Ibid., pp. 104, 115.
2. Ibid., pp. 112, 115.
3. Raymond Moody, *The Light Beyond* (New York: Bantam, 1988), p. 136.
4. Sabom, p. 155.

According to Melvin Morse, out-of-body perceptions indicate that the brain activity at the Sylvian fissure cannot explain near-death experiences. He concludes that the human being must be a soul or spirit being and that the Sylvian fissure is the true seat of the soul, a kind of interface between physical and spiritual existence. If he is correct, then not only the Sylvian fissure but the nervous system as a whole would appear to be the instrument of the soul. All the many different conditions described so far would then be site-specific modulations of the instrument of consciousness that correspond to specific alterations in the conditions of consciousness itself.

We have touched on Wilder Penfield's contributions to scientific knowledge, and Sabom takes particular note of the famous neurosurgeon's earnest and lifelong struggle with the mind-body problem. "Mind comes into action and goes out of action with the highest brain mechanism, it is true," wrote Penfield, "but the mind has energy. The form of that energy is different from that of neuronal potentials that travel the axone pathways. There I must leave it."[1] Albert Einstein's conviction that a person "who is seriously involved in the pursuit of science becomes convinced that a spirit is manifest in the laws of the Universe" also resonates with Sabom. He concludes his book by saying that the lives and deaths of the persons he came to know in his hospital deeply moved him to a sense of awe and humility before the mystery of human life.[2]

---

1. Penfield, pp. 48, 85.
2. Sabom, p. 186.

RUDOLF STEINER

THERE IS MORE TO THIS mystery of life than we have discussed so far. In our time, physicists no longer talk about the cosmos as a great machine the way Newton did; as they describe it, the cosmos looks more and more like weaving thought.[1] The work of Penfield and Sabom also points in that direction, and so we cannot leave the mystery of near-death experiences until we have considered it from nonmaterialistic points of view.

In particular, Rudolf Steiner's observations add an entirely new and challenging dimension to our investigation of near-death experiences. Readers unfamiliar with his work may appreciate some basic biographical information. Rudolf Steiner was born in 1861 to an Austrian Catholic family in Kraljevic, a small town that was then in Hungary but belongs now to Yugoslavia. His father was a telegraph operator for the Austrian railway, and later he was promoted to the position of station-master of a series of small railroad stations in Lower Austria. There the boy grew up under the influence of the deep beauty of the rural Austrian countryside. Rudolf Steiner was educated in the technical secondary school and at the Polytechnic Institute of Vienna. There his principal studies were mathematics, biology, physics, and chemistry, but classes with Karl Julius Schröer, a professor of German, interested him particularly and led to his appointment as editor of Goethe's writings on the natural sciences for a new edition of Goethe's complete works. Steiner received his doctorate in philosophy in Rostock, Germany, on completion of his dissertation on the epistemology of Fichte. He met Friedrich

---

1. Arthur Koestler, *The Roots of Coincidence* (New York: Random House, 1972), p. 58.

Nietzsche at the end of that respected philosopher's life, and in 1895 Steiner published a book on him and his philosophy. Between that time and the turn of the century, Rudolf Steiner was developing on the basis of his own creative inner vision a sense for the thought-world as shadow of a supersensible or spiritual world that people share and live in together, though for the most part they are not conscious of it.[1] In his autobiography and his other works Rudolf Steiner explains that he consciously experienced ideas as revelations of spiritual, i.e., body-free, existence. He referred to the results of his discoveries in this domain as spiritual science.

Spiritual Science and the Mind-Body Problem

What light does Rudolf Steiner's spiritual science shed on near-death experiences? To begin with, Steiner talks about what he calls the etheric world or realm of the life-forces. He distinguishes lifeless and living things by pointing out the difference we can directly sense, albeit only vaguely, between something organic, such as a plant, and something inorganic, like a stone or a piece of glass. Steiner speaks of an etheric or life body — a spiritual entity that actively participates in the formation of the cells and the metabolic processes of living things.

According to Steiner, in the human being this entity is further elaborated by thinking and develops as a tapestry of memories, judgments, and other thoughts. Over time this makes up the temperament, character, and habits of the individual. Steiner describes this etheric organization of the human being as a supersensible shape or aura of light the color of peach blossoms.[2]

In addition to the physical and etheric realms, Rudolf Steiner speaks of an astral world. The astral organization, he explains, manifests and works physically only in animals and human beings. According to Steiner, the astral body expresses itself in the development of nerve tissue, in sensation, consciousness, and will. In the human being, feelings enter into a

---

1. Rudolf Steiner, *The Course of My Life,* vol. 28 in the Collected Works (Hudson, NY: Anthroposophic Press, 1986).
2. For a bibliography on these points see Adolf Arenson, *Leitfaden durch fünfzig Vortragszyklen Rudolf Steiners* (Stuttgart: Verlag Freies Geistesleben, 1985), p. 15.

relationship with the whole individuality and are raised to the level of symbolic dreams as well as artistic and ethical impulses. Rudolf Steiner compares the appearance of the astral body for spiritual vision to a sea of light shapes that change as quickly as a person's thoughts and feelings do.

As Steiner explains, the etheric organization remains closely bound to the physical body until death while the astral body and the individuality — which are closely connected during life — are freed from the physical-etheric unity during sleep. They separate partially in the dream state and completely in dreamless sleep.[1]

It should be noted here that Rudolf Steiner's descriptions of the etheric and astral organizations are by no means unprecedented; there are ancient philosophies and religions that substantially agree with his views. For example, Indian Vedanta philosophy speaks of a physical body (*annamaya kosha*) and its supersensible double or vital sheath (*pranamaya kosha*) as well as of an astral body (*sukshma sharira*) that separates completely from the physical body at death.[2]

According to Rudolf Steiner the physical-etheric unity is severed partially and temporarily under near-death conditions, and completely and permanently at death. Concerning the near-death state, he speaks about a contemporary of his, the anthropologist and criminologist Moritz Benedikt, who saw a vast panorama of his life pass before his eyes when he nearly drowned.[3] Steiner indicates that Benedikt perceived the panorama because the etheric organization, the agent of memory, had freed itself from the resistance of the physical body, thus allowing a tableau of etheric memory pictures to rise up to consciousness. The freed etheric body was interpenetrated by the astral light of consciousness and made it possible for Benedikt to recall the experience afterwards. Steiner emphasizes that the etheric brain must be loosened from the body for this etheric tableau to occur, not because the etheric brain is the seat of memory — Steiner describes the entire etheric body as an organ of memory —

---

1. See, for example, Rudolf Steiner, *An Outline of Occult Science,* vol. 13 in the Collected Works, 3rd ed., repr. (Hudson, NY: Anthroposophic Press, 1989), ch. 3.
2. This concept is still found in Yoga philosophy today; see Swami Vishnudevananda, *The Complete Illustrated Book of Yoga* (New York: Simon & Schuster, 1974), p. 15. The etheric organization was also a clearly defined concept in many other ancient cultures; see G. B. Walker, ed., *Encyclopedia of Esoteric Man* (London: Routledge & Kegan Paul, 1977), p. 7.
3. Steiner, *Occult Science,* ch. 3.

but because the bond of the etheric body to the physical brain impedes the perception of the etheric pictures.[1]

Locating the blocking of perception at the interface between the etheric and physical brain is consistent with Steiner's observation that the etheric organization has the same shape as the physical head in the head region but is looser and vaguer around the chest and nebulous in the abdomen and limbs, where it no longer follows the contours of the body at all.[2]

How do Rudolf Steiner's insights relate to the mind-body problem? Clearly, he does not ignore the physiological aspects of the question; yet, he indicates strongly that the mind and body are separate but interdependent real entities. Similarly, the scientific observations and discoveries discussed above do not suggest that only the physiological processes are real and that the mind is merely an imagined phenomenon. We know that the direction of our attention and mental activity influences our physiological processes, just as the latter affect our mental experience.

For example, we have seen the highly specific effects natural endorphins and hallucinogenic drugs can have in this regard, and there are of course any number of other examples. Affective disorders, such as depression, exemplify chemical imbalances in the brain that can have a profound effect on a person's mental state. But we also know that an electroencephalograph shows clearly more varied patterns and more electrical activity in the brain of a musically inclined person listening to the counterpoint and the melody of a Bach sonata than we find in people listening only casually to the melody alone.

The one-sidedness of a totally physiological view of consciousness becomes evident when it is taken to its logical conclusion in such a context and people wonder why the unique patterns of electricity in the brain of trained musicians should cause them to focus on the counterpoint in addition to listening to the melody. On the other hand, a reductive,

1. Rudolf Steiner, *At the Gates of Spiritual Science,* vol. 95 in the Collected Works, repr. (London: Rudolf Steiner Press, 1970), lecture of August 24, 1906.
2. Rudolf Steiner, *Anthroposophical Leading Thoughts,* vol. 26 in the Collected Works, repr. (London: Rudolf Steiner Press, 1985), leading thoughts 32-34. The fact that according to Steiner only the head of the etheric body is clearly formed suggests a consistent feature in the phenomenon of autoscopic hallucinations discussed above, in which the shadowy image of a head and little more of the body appears, and it also suggests a spiritual basis for such experiences.

fundamentalist theology that ignores the role of the physical facts of nature is equally insufficient. We are, after all, more complex than that and constituted more subtly and delicately.

Let us now return to Wilder Penfield administering a mild electric shock to the temporal lobe of the brain and consider his results within the framework of Steiner's description of the relationship between the etheric and the physical brain. It is conceivable that direct electrical stimulation of the brain could cause the etheric organization Steiner describes to separate from the body. The scientific discoveries discussed above could be revealing a secret of human life; the same thing could occur in each instance, whether the injury involved a lack of oxygen in the blood, heart failure, drowning, suffocation from smoke inhalation, or fear of imminent death. The ancient idea of baptism as an initiation by near drowning is particularly interesting in light of Rudolf Steiner's observation that the physical and etheric bodies separated much more easily in the remote past than they do in our time.

In summary, many different kinds of influences seem to interact in near-death experiences. Apparently, physiological considerations dominate in the initial stages of NDEs. For example, researchers have proposed that the buzzing sound at the onset of the experience could be related to unusual electrical activity in Heschl's gyrus[1] and that the tunnel image could well be an abnormal experience of the retina.[2]

The activity at the Sylvian fissure, however, poses an entirely different sort of problem. The relationship between electrical stimulation of this site in the brain and visions of the dead or other incorporeal beings leads us beyond the limits of our ordinary intellect. Sabom's study indicates that our consciousness is sufficiently independent of our physiology to accurately apprehend physical details of the environment in the near-death state and to recall them later. However, this independence is not sufficient to allow our consciousness to escape the effect of drugs administered to the body during the near-death experience.[3] More specific conclusions

---

1. Sabom, p. 174.
2. See Susan Blackmore's essay "Out of the Body?" in Robert Basil, ed., *Not Necessarily the New Age* (Buffalo: Prometheus Books, 1988) p. 172.
3. Sabom, 170.

that go beyond individual experience are not yet possible. Autoscopy, however, the moment of viewing the body from above or from one side, brings us face to face with the riddle of consciousness.

Here we return to George Ritchie's account of his near-death experience, which has led to the recent scientific and public interest in the phenomenon of near-death experiences. Ritchie's account helps us explore the question more deeply since it is not only particularly well documented but also broader in scope and more exactly detailed than other comparable recent reports of near-death experiences.

PART TWO

THE NEAR-DEATH EXPERIENCE
OF DR. GEORGE G. RITCHIE, JR.

THE NEAR-DEATH EXPERIENCE
OF DR. GEORGE G. RITCHIE, JR.

ALL OF US CAN point to decisive events and meetings in our lives. George Ritchie underwent the decisive experience of his life in 1943.[1] In the winter of that year, he was a twenty-year-old recruit in basic training at Camp Barkeley, a remote army outpost in Texas. He had almost completed basic training when on Thanksgiving afternoon, with understandable trepidation, he had to report to a regimental board. Their announcement: "We have decided to send you to the Medical College of Virginia to study medicine." Arrangements were to be made in the following weeks.

It was bitterly cold that December, and George Ritchie came down with an infection of the upper respiratory tract. Many of the other recruits were sick as well, and a number of them developed pneumonia and died. Ritchie's infection became serious while he was in the camp hospital. On December 19, Ritchie found himself in the recuperation ward, tremendously excited, waiting to be picked up by jeep the following morning at 4:30 A.M. He would be on his way to Abilene to catch the train to Richmond, Virginia. That evening a friend joined him to celebrate the great event with a trip to the movies. They went to the early show since Ritchie would have to get up the next morning at 3 o'clock.

Four months earlier, George Ritchie had been a premedical student at the University of Richmond, selected to attend the Medical College of

---

1. George G. Ritchie, *Return From Tomorrow* (Old Tappan, New Jersey: Fleming Revell, 1978).

Virginia. He would have been one of the youngest ever to graduate there, at the age of twenty-two. But, in Ritchie's words, "man proposes, and God disposes."

When he returned from the movies, he knew something was very wrong. He felt ill and hot, but he was not about to notify the doctors. Classes were to start on December 22 in Richmond, and if he wasn't there, someone else would gladly take his place. A cold was not going to stop him from taking the next great step in his life. He asked the ward boy, a friend of his, for six aspirin tablets and three APC tablets; he took two of each and went to bed. At 2:00 A.M. on December 20, he woke up feeling worse. He turned on the light, and when he saw the sputum cup with blood in it, he became alarmed. He asked the ward boy for a thermometer. His temperature was 106.5 degrees. He realized it was a wonder that he was still rational.

Ritchie knew he was in trouble, and this time he called the nurse. Soon a doctor was by his side who suspected immediately that the respiratory tract infection had developed into life-threatening pneumonia. Twenty minutes before the arrival of the jeep for Abilene, an ambulance came to take him for X rays at the hospital instead. "Private Ritchie, can you stand up to take an X ray?" He replied, "What a silly question, of course I can." That was his last memory before he regained consciousness on Christmas Eve.[1]

Early on the morning of December 21, the day before classes began at the medical school in Richmond, the ward boy found George Ritchie not only unconscious but also without any pulse, respiration, or blood pressure. The doctor of osteopathy arrived and verified the ward boy's tests and pronounced George Ritchie dead. "When you finish your rounds, prep him for the morgue," he told the ward boy.

---

1. The particularly careful reader will note that this last memory from ordinary experience appears to mix into the near-death experience itself at that moment when the figure of light appears and the words "Stand up" form in Ritchie's mind. This may be a mixed or subjective coloring to the experience, but, again, it may not be. The work of depth psychology concerning the significance of puns and literal meanings of words indicates that these often convey deeply meaningful associations. The phrase "stand up" conveys as a verb the state of being upright — which means to be conscientious or morally responsible. And this is the essence of the better self that makes its appearance in so many people during the NDE.

According to the hospital records, the ward boy returned nine minutes after Ritchie was first pronounced dead to get the body ready for the morgue. He did not do that, however; he was sure the body had moved in the meantime, and so he ran back to get the doctor again. The check for vital signs was again conclusive, and George Ritchie was again pronounced dead. Strangely enough, this was the only case among all the deaths at the camp where a ward boy refused to accept the authority of his superior officer. Although it was unthinkable for an untrained ward boy to question an officer, especially a licensed physician, this one begged the doctor to give Ritchie a shot of adrenalin to the heart.

The physician knew that this was not a useful practice in cases where the vital organs had deteriorated from disease. He surprised himself, however, when instead of rebuking the boy he acceded to his wish. He injected adrenalin into George Ritchie's heart, and his heart began to beat again, at first erratically, then steadily. He began to breathe, and his pulse rose progressively. Dr. Donald G. Francy, the commanding officer to whom the doctor of osteopathy had made his reports, called Ritchie's survival "the most amazing medical case [I] had ever encountered" and said that it had to be "explained in terms of other than natural means."[1] Let us now turn to George Ritchie's account of the nine minutes he spent in the near-death state.

The Nine Minutes

George Ritchie tells of finding himself suddenly looking at his body in the hospital room from above, filled with panic; he calls this the greatest shock of his life. He relates that he maddeningly found himself floating through walls and doors and even people. He felt an icy loneliness settling over him that he says cannot be comprehended in terms of bodily experiences at all. Given Michael Sabom's accounts of patients' apparently accurate observation of the surroundings under such conditions, it becomes apparent that the concept of out-of-body experiences merits serious attention. Rudolf Steiner's treatment of this subject also touches on the feeling of loneliness Ritchie describes.

---

1. Ritchie, p. 81.

According to Steiner, there are two separate but related modes of the body-free faculty, or astral organization as he calls it. He describes the astral body as essentially a spiritual fountain of light in the spiritual world. Imaginatively speaking, only the rays of this entity extend into the time-space of earth life.[1] However, as Steiner explains, the astrality of the incarnate human being, the astral aura, does not readily remain true to the laws of the astral world because it is chained to the sensory impressions and memories of daily experience.[2]

When we apply Rudolf Steiner's explanation to Ritchie's experience, it would appear that in awakening inside the earthly astral body, the individual experiences a totally unfamiliar state of alienation and confusion concerning the material world and feels chained to it as to an unnoticed shadow. At the same time, he or she does not yet perceive anything in the spiritual world because his or her soul has not yet become acclimated to its laws. This description applies to near-death and out-of-body experiences. And George Ritchie describes his own experiences in just such somber terms — up to the moment of his encounter with Christ.

The Life-Review or Etheric Tableau

George Ritchie reports that the dark hospital room then began to light up all around him until it was bathed in an indescribably dazzling brilliance. At that point, what appeared to him as the shape of a man of light stepped toward him from out of the light. This figure of light stood by his side while a panorama of his life passed before his eyes in complete detail, and all the thoughts of his mind were laid open to this figure, whom he now calls his guide.

Interestingly enough, this experience of the illuminated past is described in precise detail in one of the most ancient extant literary documents, the *Brihadaranyaka Upanishad* of India. According to this book, the human being lives after death "only in the subtle body, on

---

1. Rudolf Steiner, *Anthroposophy: An Introduction*, vol. 234 in the Collected Works (London: Rudolf Steiner Press, 1983), pp. 74-75.
2. See Rudolf Steiner, *The Threshold of the Spiritual World* and *The Road to Self-Knowledge*, vol. 17 in the Collected Works, 3d ed., repr. (London: Rudolf Steiner Press, 1975), pp. 43, 44.

which are left the impressions of his past deeds, and of these impressions he is aware, illumined as they are by the pure light of the Self."[1] Similarly, Rudolf Steiner explains that the individuality enters into overflowing clear light and heightened awareness when the etheric organization is freed at death,[2] and that during the next few days the individual sees the life that just ended pass before him or her in a tableau of brightly illuminated pictures that expand and then become thin and fade. In this process, the spiritual beings of the stars receive the thoughts, feelings, intentions, and actions that nourished life on earth, and reject those that did not.[3] In view of this, the obvious question is whether the near-death experience is a foretaste of the far-reaching afterlife scenario Rudolf Steiner describes, and we will approach this issue from as many perspectives as possible.

The Light of Conscience and the Guardian of the Threshold

In his numerous works, Rudolf Steiner speaks of the subtler aspects of this event. He explained that at death our conscience is revealed in the etheric organization as the cosmic light by which we perceive and judge the ethical value of our past life.[4] If our conscience is indeed more than a behaviorally conditioned set of social norms, if it is in fact a faculty of the soul independent of the body, then Sabom, Ritchie, and Steiner may have an answer to the mind-body problem. Clearly, studies of near-death experiences corroborate that the life-review, when it does take place, is sensed as a divine judgment or self-judgment, and these are certainly attributes of any definition of conscience.

George Ritchie and many others who have been confronted by the conscience as an elemental force of condemnation in near-death experiences say that they were near despair when their self-image and pride

1. Swami Prabhavananda and F. Manchester, trans., *The Upanishads: Breath of the Eternal* (New York: New American Library), p. 105.
2. Rudolf Steiner, *Das Geheimnis des Todes*, vol. 159/160 in the Collected Works (Dornach, Switzerland: Rudolf Steiner Verlag, 1963), p. 327.
3. See *Anthroposophy: An Introduction*, vol. 234 in the Collected Works, lecture of February 10, 1924 (London: Rudolf Steiner Press, 1983).
4. Rudolf Steiner, *Supersensible Man*, vol. 231 in the Collected Works (London: Anthroposophical Publishing Co., 1961), lecture of November 13, 1923.

unraveled in the accusing light of their conscience. However, Rudolf Steiner contributes a remarkable insight about the quality of this despair at the gate of death. He relates it to an impending extinction of the everyday self at the threshold of the spiritual world and thus to the first stage of the archetypal death-rebirth experience many ancient cultures have clothed in countless myths. The spiritual world destroys anything that is bound to the laws of the material world, just as antibodies locate viruses in the bloodstream for other proteins of the immune system to destroy. In this way, almost all the psychological foundations of the self become a target to be shredded at the threshold to the spiritual world. The first assault comes from the self's moral faculty or conscience, which takes on the stature of a godlike accuser and tormentor. In addition, Steiner noted that the majestic animal or dragon figures hewn in stone that guard the thresholds of the ancient world's gates, temples, and tombs also stand watch at the gate of death. They are, in fact, archetypal images of this cosmic moral law. For example, the Egyptians believed that lion-gods guarded the gates of morning and evening; the Greeks came to call this creature the sphinx. The famous sphinx at Gizeh is an image of the sun-god Ra-Temu-Khepera-Herukhuti.[1] In this context, we may recall the Near Eastern story describing the trembling human soul at the gate of death, watching a god or gods place his heart on one side of a scales against a feather on the other. Plato's story about Er, which was recounted in the beginning of this book, also mentions judges seated in the space between the openings of earth and heaven where Er's near-death experience began.

According to Steiner, the approach of such a guardian at the gate of death is inescapable, but its appearance is fleeting and often goes unnoticed.[2] While George Ritchie describes qualities of what Steiner calls the guardian of the threshold, he did not describe its outward appearance. Descriptions of the guardian of the threshold are relatively common in accounts of near-death experiences. For example, a boy who was nearly killed when a power line touched the tree he was climbing

---

1. Elisabeth E. Goldsmith, *Ancient Pagan Symbols* (New York: Putnam, 1929), p. 118.
2. Rudolf Steiner, *Man in the Light of Occultism*, vol. 137 in the Collected Works (London: Rudolf Steiner Press, 1964), lecture of June 10, 1912.

describes an encounter with such a guardian. According to his report of his near-death experience, he first wandered through a frightening and mythic forest, feeling very lonely. Then he met a terrifying figure covered with scars and serpents.[1] Here, as in many other accounts, only the guardian's dreadful and frightening aspects are experienced and none of its lionlike majesty and archangelic perfection that Steiner describes.

According to Rudolf Steiner, the guardian of the threshold holds up a mirror to the hidden ugliness and shame within the human being.[2] When confronted with the guardian of the threshold, the self perceives predominantly those personal aspects that must be torn to shreds and discarded at the threshold to the spiritual world rather than the majesty of the guardian. George Ritchie, too, experienced the guardian of the threshold as an existential self-accusation, making him feel that his life had been a series of mistakes.

As Rudolf Steiner explains, the guardian of the threshold to the spiritual world is at work in the soul's experiences during dreamless sleep and manifests in the moral impulses we have in our waking life even though we are usually not aware of it.[3] Thus, what happens unconsciously every night when we fall asleep finally happens consciously and irrevocably at death (or it can happen by way of initiation) — in other words, our whole sense-bound self-image feels its impending, complete, and permanent obliteration at the threshold to the spiritual world. Our reaction to the details of this scenario is significant in itself. Our concept of mind and consciousness is affected by how we understand this so-called guardian of the threshold, by whether we relegate it to the realm of phantasms, putting it on equal footing with the shadow-gestalt of C. G. Jung's psychology, or whether we sense it is part of a spiritual reality like the one Rudolf Steiner describes.

---

1. Amy S. Genova, "The Near Death Experience," *McCall's*, February, 1988, p. 106.
2. Rudolf Steiner, *Initiation, Eternity and the Passing Moment*, vol. 138 in the Collected Works (Spring Valley, NY: Anthroposophic Press, 1980), lecture of August 27, 1912.
3. Rudolf Steiner, *The Etherisation of the Blood*, vol. 130 in the Collected Works (London: Rudolf Steiner Press, 1971), lecture of October 1, 1911; *The Bridge Between Universal Spirituality and the Physical Constitution of Man*, from vol. 202 in the Collected Works, repr. (Spring Valley, NY: Anthroposophic Press, 1979).

Moses and Christ and the Judgment of Souls

Many people who survive close brushes with death report having seen a radiant light or a being of radiant light, and they identify the latter as their higher or better self; some even describe meeting a radiant angel or God. According to Rudolf Steiner's spiritual investigations, the results of which are outlined above, the experience of the first group can be described as a vision of the spiritual light of the etheric self, which is our conscience, and that of the second group can be called a meeting with the guardian of the threshold. In particular, Steiner identifies the guardian of the threshold as an archangel.[1] However, George Ritchie and others claim that the being of light they met was definitely Christ himself. This does not contradict Steiner's findings concerning the spiritual world; rather, it fits in with another of his perceptions, which can fruitfully be applied to near-death experiences. According to Steiner, in our time two beings in particular help the soul that is freed of the body during the illumination and judgment of the life review tableau at the threshold to the spiritual world:

> Just before the period of purification in the soul world [just before purgatory begins] a special event takes place. . . . A meeting takes place between the human being and a very special being who holds before him the register of his past deeds. And this individual, who stands there as a kind of bookkeeper of the karmic powers, has been for many the figure of Moses. . . . This office, however, is changing hands in the course of our age — and this is a highly significant matter — and toward the end of the twentieth century the human being will ever more frequently encounter Christ Jesus as the judge of karma.[2]

This raises the question whether Steiner envisions the life-review experience as a single event involving both the illumination of conscience at the threshold and the judgment of Moses or Christ, or whether he treats these as two separate events. Our first inclination is to think that

---

1. Rudolf Steiner, *Initiation, Eternity and the Passing Moment*, p. 65.
2. Rudolf Steiner, *From Jesus to Christ*, vol. 131 in the Collected Works (London: Rudolf Steiner Press, 1973), lecture of October 7, 1911.

he is likely speaking of a single event, given the obvious connection between the notion of the self-judging conscience and Moses as the Western world's archetypal guardian of ethical dictates. Indeed, this turns out to have been Steiner's intention. The judgment encounter with Moses or Christ takes place "just before the period of purification in the soul world."[1]

Rudolf Steiner calls this period of purification *kamaloca* or purgatory. During this period, the astral body from the past life is laid aside and largely dissolved into the astral world. This event is the astral parallel to the etheric panoramic life review of *conscious* experience; it involves, however, only those events that were *lost to our consciousness* during sleep in our life on earth. Kamaloca lasts for about a third of our earthly lifetime; it is preceded by the unfolding of the etheric tableau, which lasts only about as long as the individual could remain awake at one stretch during life on earth, about two or three days. Obviously, then, the emergence of the etheric conscience and the cooperation of Moses or Christ in the tableau of self-judgment take place within the period of a few hours or days.

How will an encounter with Moses during the life review differ from one with Christ? Let us now look to other sources to see whether they confirm or disprove his characterization of the relationship of Moses and Christ to the human soul.[2]

To begin with, we can consider the Old Testament image of Moses as a majestic judge bringing down the Ten Commandments from Mt. Sinai. He brought his people the laws of conscience and of the spiritual-moral world engraved in stone. This image of Moses as a spiritual judge or the embodiment of spiritual law contrasts sharply with that of Christ Jesus as merciful and forgiving. The contrast between these two images echoes the statement in the Gospel of John that "the law was given through Moses; grace and truth came through Jesus Christ" (John 1:17).

The grace and forgiveness Jesus brings are illustrated in the story of the adulteress in this same Gospel. The scribes and Pharisees want to stone

---

1. Ibid.
2. See Rudolf Steiner, *Reincarnation and Karma*, vol. 135 in the Collected Works (North Vancouver: Steiner Book Centre, 1977), lecture of February 20, 1912.

her to death in accordance with the letter of the law of Moses as they understand it. When they try to enlist Jesus' cooperation, he refuses to condemn her and tells them, "Let him who is without sin among you be the first to throw a stone at her" (John 8:7). Here, Christ works as the judge of souls in an unexpected way, speaking directly to the conscience of each stone-wielding Pharisee and scribe. After he has thus called them to examine their own conscience, they all drop their stones and leave. Jesus also wrote something in the sand at the woman's feet, an action that is reminiscent of the writing on Moses' tablets. Jesus here is the judge of the soul as well as the guide; the judgment of this woman's innermost spiritual nature inscribed in the sand at her feet, compels her in a way that allows no deceit or self-justification to face the moral condition of her soul. Yet, throughout this encounter, Jesus never reproaches or condemns the woman. It is understandable, then, that Rudolf Steiner also refers to Christ as the second or greater guardian of the threshold, the lion of Judah, whose being encompasses and yet transcends the first guardian's fearful aspect.

Another time, in the Sermon on the Mount, Jesus counseled his followers, "Judge not, that you be not judged. For with the judgment you pronounce you will be judged, and the measure you give will be the measure you get" (Matthew 7:1-2). Jesus healed people even on the sabbath, whether the scribes liked it or not; his word for them was "Woe to you lawyers! for you have taken away the key of knowledge; you did not enter yourselves, and you hindered those who were entering" (Luke 11:52).

Nevertheless, according to his own statements, Jesus does not oppose the laws of Moses. In the Sermon on the Mount Jesus tells the crowds, "Think not that I have come to abolish the law and the prophets; I have come not to abolish them but to fulfil them. For truly, I say to you, till heaven and earth pass away, not an iota, not a dot, will pass from the law until all is accomplished" (Matthew 5:17-18). Also, at the Transfiguration, Moses, the giver of the law, stands in the light at one side of the Transfigured Christ.

The issue of judgment and forgiveness takes on an added dimension when we view the law of Moses as an ideal realm not identical with the scribes' narrow conception of it, which was limited to the letter of the law. We can focus on the spirit of the law, particularly in connection with the life review in near-death experiences as well as with the guardian of the threshold and the judgment of souls portrayed in the ancient religions and described in detail by Steiner.

The seeming paradox between Christ's judgment of the soul and his forgiving love is central to George Ritchie's account of his near-death experience. On the one hand, he reports an illumination of his conscience that revealed his every fault as well as the bitterness, regret, embarrassment, and shame of the fallible personality. On the other hand, he also experiences a special sense of belonging, wholeness, and promise in the compassion flowing from the being of light. Thus, his experience is characterized by the presence of Moses in the severe and accusing light directed upon the conscience and of Christ in the grace and love streaming toward the soul.

> I realized that it was I who was judging the events around us so harshly. It was I who saw them as trivial, self-centered, unimportant. No such condemnation came from the Glory shining round me. He was not blaming or reproaching. He was simply . . . loving me.[1]

Rudolf Steiner was also acutely aware of the seeming paradox between law and grace, as his descriptions of the judgment of souls at the gate of death and of the different functions of Moses and Christ clearly show. As Christ increasingly takes on the role of lord of human destiny, the tension between his status as judge of souls and the substance of grace he brings to the world will emerge with ever greater clarity. Steiner illuminated the apparent contradiction between Moses' law and Christ's grace from many different perspectives. He saw the revelation of moral judgment and the process of the dispensation of grace — apparently contradictory processes — as parallel expressions of the same moral being of the world:

> Love appears on earth in the East; conscience in the West. The two belong together. As Christ appears in the East, so conscience awakens in the West that through it Christ may be received. In the simultaneous occurrence and comprehension of the fact of the

---

1. Ritchie, p. 54.

Christ event, and in the preparation for these things in different parts of the earth, we see the rule of an infinite wisdom guiding our development.[1]

This insight is echoed by the words "Let the East fire what the West crystallizes into shape and form" from Rudolf Steiner's *Foundation Stone* meditation.[2] Steiner viewed the Mosaic and Roman laws as institutions that would lead to a completely rigid, materialistic culture if the spiritual vitality of the East could not be integrated in the right way, and he pointed to St. Paul's experience of the light of the risen Christ near Damascus as a turning point in the history of the Greco-Roman world. "As long as mankind was not ready to follow the law inwardly," Steiner once noted, "as long as man was under a yoke, and the Rod of Moses was present in the law, so long would the law lie in the Ark of the Covenant; until the Pauline principle, the principle of grace came to man . . . when love has united with the law, and this is grace."[3]

Rudolf Steiner and the Rose-Cross

Taken together, the New Testament, George Ritchie and Rudolf Steiner tell an intricately crafted, richly textured, and multifaceted story. Moreover, the story retains a peculiar dynamic tension, a certain element of paradox, through each retelling that rings true.

Rudolf Steiner indicates that elements of paradox lie at the foundation of existence and that they can be grasped intuitively. He speaks of a symbol of the issue at hand, the contemplation of which may lead into the living reality of this paradox: the rose-cross. The symbol begins as a dark cross from whose intersection a circle of seven radiant red roses grows.[4] The essence of this image can also be found in the legend of Tannhäuser's staff. Tannhäuser leaves the Venusberg and makes a pilgrimage to Rome.

---

1. Rudolf Steiner, *The Christ Impulse and the Development of Ego Consciousness,* vol. 116 in the Collected Works (Spring Valley, NY: Anthroposophic Press, 1976), pp. 132-133.
2. Rudolf Steiner, *The Christmas Conference for the Foundation of the Anthroposophical Society, 1923/24,* vol. 260 in the Collected Works (Hudson, NY: Anthroposophic Press, 1990).
3. Rudolf Steiner, *The Temple Legend,* vol. 93 in the Collected Works (London: Rudolf Steiner Press, 1985), pp. 175-176.
4. See Steiner, *Occult Science,* ch. 5.

The Pope tells Tannhäuser that he is as likely to be pardoned as the dead staff he is leaning on is likely to sprout into bloom — upon which the staff does begin to bloom. This symbol illuminates the mystery of the Transfiguration or of a meeting with Christ, such as the one Ritchie experienced.

The reality symbolized here could be described as follows. Our conscience can be seen as a cross in harsh light. Its right angles become the standards against which all the soul's past thoughts, feelings, and actions are measured. The thoughts, feelings, and actions that failed to nourish the world drive the soul into a state of anxiety and narrow isolation; there is as little place for these in the spiritual order of things as there is for the intention of a branch or rock to defy gravity in the natural world. Consequently, the soul feels emptied of its being. In the recesses of its memory, the soul dreads throughout life the threshold that waits to receive or reject the many images that make up its past. Throughout life, the soul feels, at least faintly, that each time it passes a judgment on others that should rightly have been reserved for itself, it becomes a stranger to itself. Even the satisfaction of righteous anger and just punishment of others for their misdeeds is shallow and empty; they inevitably distort the true face of the soul.

In contemplating the image of the rose-cross in an attempt to understand its import, we begin to sense that our conscience, though often causing us anxiety and pain, is more than a cruel judge. It is also a less and less passive external and more and more an active and inward power of our individuality; it knows that the debts and mistakes the soul must account for to the last farthing are also dark, fertile soil for something higher. Even in our everyday life we can sense that wholeness dawns behind our memories of moments when our soul forgot itself, so to speak, and attended directly to the needs of others, whether we were lending a hand, working on a needed project, or creating a work of art. Behind such memories the soul begins to expand into states of renewed certainty and serenity. It experiences a sunrise that promises to bring to flowering what was dead, wooden law.

We can test whether our own lives contain such moments by observing the role love and friendship play in our lives. Are they gratefully received and serve the soul as nourishment for productive living, or are they sought instead as a diversion, as armor of an illusory self-validation to repress the judgment of the self within us? In one case we can live in peace with ourselves and others; in the other we are driven by self-torment and torment others by trying to manipulate them. Most of us live somewhere between these two extremes.

If the dead hand of the law completely rules our lives, they turn into a mechanical drudgery of perfectionism and self-doubt. We then begin to ward off the approach of grace. On the surface, this may take the form of refusing a compliment for work well done by saying, "It was nothing." On a more fundamental, existential level, we may simply not feel "good enough" to receive, or even to allow ourselves to want to receive, the gift of something purer and higher than ourselves. Consequently, good fortune and loving relationships may make us uneasy or even cause us to feel guilty. We may then feed on the manipulation of blame, seeking out the weak points in others to chastise, influence, and otherwise manipulate them. The result is, of course, that we become unable to cooperate and share with others; our lives become ever more bitterly trivial, formal, and empty. Alternatively, this basic sense of unworthiness may prompt us to try to make others feel the sting of conscience for not pandering to our infirmities. As long as we are allowing ourselves to be driven by these patterns, we cannot be truly free.

We all tend to resist change and to tell and retell our self-justifying stories, explaining and at once exonerating the way we are. With each telling we postpone the inevitable appointment with the judge within. Though the changes this judge would have us make are for our own benefit, they involve a kind of death of the old self, and therefore we dread them. However, if we can bring ourselves to hear the inner judge's truth, to accept it, and to give ourselves over to the process of change and transformation into a better, higher self, life can becomes as fascinating and absorbing as creating a work of art; our life can then become a blessing and force of change for others.

As the above-mentioned New Testament passages and also the reports of Steiner and Ritchie indicate, to allow grace and truth to flow freely into our lives, we have to take the laws into ourselves and make them into our conscience. In other words, we have to have the courage to carry out the judging function of Moses ourselves, and in the process we will meet

Christ. In the metaphysical sense, it is no longer healthy or appropriate to meet Moses descending from Mount Sinai with the stone tablets; instead, we now have to look for him at the side of the transfigured Christ.

Vessel of the Suprapersonal

Both George Ritchie and Rudolf Steiner describe a second fundamental quality of Christ that is essential to an understanding of the Transfiguration. We have spoken about the guardian of the threshold to the spiritual world and about the shame and regret the soul feels over personal mistakes and character flaws in the presence of the guardian. Steiner also talks about a second, higher guardian in the spiritual world whose task goes beyond the improvement and perfection of the individual. This being remains unfulfilled as long as human souls suffer in the world. This being is Christ, and when he appears to a human soul at the threshold to the spiritual world, he asks for more than an accounting for personal errors and flaws. He asks for an accounting of what deeds of love we have freely done to nourish the world.

Ritchie describes that when he held out his successes in life to the overwhelming presence that asked him what worth his life had had, the Christ being seemed to reply, albeit gently and lovingly, "That glorified you." In essence, Ritchie's offer was a gift that he himself had already received, whether by destiny or grace. As he put it in his report of his near-death experience, he felt as if questions on a branch of study in which his college did not offer any courses had been added to his final examination. For the Christ-like being, the special meaning of a life consists, aside from abstention from serious moral transgressions, in positive deeds of selfless love that nourish the world. Certainly, the truth of the laws contained in the Ten Commandments is transparent to many people, but the gravity of passing by an opportunity to extend loving attention to someone or to eradicate a social injustice is not equally apparent. In a sense, we have here two clearly distinct spheres of moral responsibility, one characterized by the figure and judgment of Moses and the other by those of Christ.

On the basis of this difference between the judgments of Moses and Christ, we can understand why the judgment by Christ so rarely takes place concurrently with that of Moses: self-love will be sufficient motivation to work on overcoming personality flaws and defects, but a higher love is needed to motivate us to deeds that nourish the world. In the language of the Transfiguration scene, the necessary self-transformation at this stage can be accomplished only when the Moses principle is completely irradiated by Christ's love. In the symbolic language of the rose-cross, the faintly bluish hue that distinguishes rose-red from red is an expression of this higher love.

It is easy to reject the notion of such a second sphere of moral responsibility by arguing that the idea of humanity is an abstraction. Nevertheless, it is a matter of eminently practical application. The characterization of our twentieth century world as a global village is accurate, and we are each part of its ecology. The consequences of short-term and exclusively profit-oriented planning in industry and agriculture are well known. The damage to the environment reveals the deadliness of our selfishness writ large. Clearly, the damage modern civilization has wrought goes far beyond the individual's capacity to feel responsible and guilty; nevertheless it is an illustration of a staggering lack of love in the world. As Rudolf Steiner once so clearly noted, love in its purest form is a gift to the world for which there is no recompense. Sadly, in democracies no less than in totalitarian states, the apparent needs of the moment drown out nearly all concern for the welfare of the generations to come.

Returning to Rudolf Steiner's portrayal of the judgments by Moses and by Christ, we begin to understand that the significance of Christ replacing Moses as the judge of souls means, in the language of anthroposophy, that the soul is beginning to meet both guardians of the threshold to the spiritual world at the moment of crossing over into the invisible worlds.

The Apocalyptic Christ

George Ritchie's description of the being of light — "out of this brilliant light stepped this form of sheer light" — a man of brilliant light who seemed to step into the room out of the surrounding brilliant light is particularly significant because of its similarity to that given by one of the characters in Rudolf Steiner's first mystery drama:

Before my spirit stands a Form in shining light,
and from it words sound forth to me.

. . . .

You have lived long in faith;
you have been comforted by hope.
So now be comforted with sight;

. . . .

A human being emerges from the radiant light
and speaks to me:
You shall proclaim to all
who have the will to hear,
that you have seen
what men shall soon experience.
The Christ once lived upon the earth,
and from this life it follows
that He encompasses as Soul
men's growth on earth.[1]

Both Steiner's and Ritchie's descriptions echo the depiction of Christ as a spirit-man moving among seven candlesticks in the *Book of Revelation*. We have to ask then how such a superhuman being could be connected with the destiny of the human race. Steiner saw finding the answer to this question as the essential task of his spiritual science or anthroposophy (Greek for "wisdom of the human being," which Steiner translates as "consciousness of one's actual humanity.")[2]

George Ritchie's narrative of his near-death experience goes to the heart of this question, as do the reports of others who have survived close encounters with death. For example, fifteen-year-old Kevin Vida, the boy mentioned above who was nearly killed by a fallen power line, also

---

1. Rudolf Steiner, *The Portal of Initiation*, vol. 14 in the Collected Works, repr. (Blauvelt, NY: Steinerbooks, 1981), p. 36.
2. Rudolf Steiner, *Awakening to Community*, vol. 257 in the Collected Works (Spring Valley, NY: Anthroposophic Press, 1974), p. 61. Rudolf Steiner came to apply the word *anthroposophy* to his teleology of the human being. He observes that the philosopher J. P. V. Troxler used this word to describe a modern philosophy in a lecture of 1835, and I. H. Fichte — the son of the famous nineteenth-century philosopher — continued its use in the twentieth century. See also Günther Wachsmuth, *Die Geburt der Geisteswissenschaft* (Dornach, Switzerland: Philosophisch-Anthroposophischer Verlag am Goetheanum, 1941), p. 12.

reports experiencing the being of light. He describes suddenly sensing warmth radiating toward him from above and looking up into a crystal-clear light brighter than the sun. "Inside the light was the figure of a man with his hand held out to me, radiating so much love. . . . It was the most beautiful feeling I've ever experienced. I never wanted to leave."[1] There are numerous accounts of encounters with Christ in the form of Jesus, and some of them suggest this stepping forth out of a circle of light. Such perceptions have occurred in near-death experiences as well as under other circumstances.[2]

The first, brilliant but amorphous light, which has been characterized above as the freed etheric body and the light of conscience, is frequently described in NDE literature, and a particular individual may or may not associate it with a higher being such as God, the Lord Jesus, or an angel. Raymond Moody, Karlis Osis, and others conclude that this identification of the light with Christ or some other deity is a culturally determined interpretation.[3] However, I suggest that while these researchers may be correct concerning the first light, they are less so when the figure of Jesus Christ is involved. In this context, Carol Zaleski correctly emphasizes that the line between immediate experience and interpretation is a fine one. By way of example, she focuses on a near-death vision reported in Ring's study. One of Ring's subjects described seeing Jesus holding a communion chalice during his near-death experience. Zaleski suggests that to view Jesus and the chalice as interpreted elements of the experience probably does away with the content of the experience altogether and leaves nothing to interpret.[4]

As we have noted, only a few persons who survive close brushes with death and report a meeting with a being of light identify this being as Jesus Christ. In fact, after six years of research, Ring found no single report in his study of the being of light identifying himself as Christ.[5] The fact that he did not come across George Ritchie's book in the course of

1. Genova, p. 103.
2. See Zaleski, p. 127; see also Gunnar Hillerdal and Berndt Gustaffson, *Sie erlebten Christus* (Basel: Die Pforte, 1980).
3. Karlis Osis and Erlendur Haraldsson, *At the Hour of Death* (New York, 1977), p. 3.
4. Zaleski, p. 127.
5. Kenneth Ring, *Heading Toward Omega* (New York: Quill, 1984), p. 87.

his research is no indictment of his study. It may be significant that Ritchie would not have recognized the cosmic, resurrected Christ on the basis of the mild image he had of him from Sunday school. Ritchie's experience is also reminiscent of the description of the meeting between Mary Magdalene and the resurrected Christ in the Gospel of John. At first, she mistook the risen Lord for a gardener. It would appear to follow that the soul can meet the higher guardian of the threshold without recognizing in him the historical person of Jesus. We expect the cosmic Christ to be the representative of all human beings, not of any single cultural or ethnic type.

The moving story of the boy who described the love of the man of crystalline light underscores the same qualities we found in Christ as Ritchie experienced him. Rudolf Steiner's insights concur with these descriptions; he stated frequently, for example, that people in great need may be consoled by a stranger, who is none other than Christ unrecognized. The New Testament touches on the other side of this mystery in teaching us that a loving deed we do for another, for any other person, even for the least among us, is done for Christ himself.

Christus, Verus Luciferus

Another aspect of the similarity between Steiner's experience of Christ and Ritchie's in his near-death experience bears mention here. Ritchie's description of his guide as a light so bright that mortal eyes would be blinded to look on him may remind us of the apocryphal ties between Christ and Lucifer—the early Christians spoke of Christ as Verus Luciferus, or the true Lucifer.[1] We cannot help wondering, then, what distinguishes the light of Christ from that of Lucifer. Ritchie's characterization of his meeting with Christ reveals the uniqueness of the person of Christ:

> This was the most totally male Being I had ever met. If this was the Son of God, then His name was Jesus. But . . . this was not the Jesus of my Sunday School books. That Jesus had been gentle,

---

1. Rudolf Steiner, *The Apocalypse of St. John*, vol. 104 in the Collected Works (London: Rudolf Steiner Press, 1977), p. 130.

kind, understanding — and probably a little bit of a weakling. This Person, however, was power itself, older than time and yet more modern than anyone I had ever met.

Far more even than power, what emanated from this Presence was unconditional love. An astonishing love. A love beyond my wildest imagining. This love knew every unlovable thing about me — the quarrels with my stepmother, my explosive temper, the sex thoughts I could never control, every mean, selfish thought and action since the day I was born — and accepted and loved me just the same.[1]

George Ritchie describes a being of limitless power, akin to the terrifying figure of flowing bronze and fire from the New Testament *Book of Revelation* or the guardian of the threshold of the ancient mysteries, a being who also appears to know everything there is to know about him.[2] Yet, despite the power Ritchie felt emanating from this being of light, he also felt a compassion pouring forth from him that exceeds even the impression of unlimited power.

Rudolf Steiner was also moved to speak of this characteristic of the highest being; as he put it, God shares his omniscience with Lucifer and his omnipotence with Satan, but unalloyed love can only come from himself alone.[3]

Church Doctrine and the Teleology of the Human Being

At the conclusion of our discussion of George Ritchie's and Rudolf Steiner's descriptions of the individuality of Christ, we should mention that neither of these men adheres to any form of fundamentalist or otherwise sectarian view of the renewal or rebirth of the human being in Christ. George Ritchie expressed surprise at finding the mild, antiquarian

---

1. Ritchie, p. 49.
2. See Rudolf Steiner, *Occult Signs and Symbols* (Spring Valley, NY: Anthroposophic Press, 1972), lecture of September 16, 1907. Incidentally, Steiner interprets the figure of fire with feet of flowing hot bronze in the *Book of Revelation* as a picture of the birth of the higher self in Christ. See also C. S. Lewis, *Mere Christianity* (New York: Macmillan, 1978), "The New Men."
3. Rudolf Steiner, *Love and Its Meaning in the World*, repr. (London: Rudolf Steiner Press, 1985).

Christ of his Sunday school days give way to a being of limitless power that would have struck terror in his heart if it had not been for the compassion he felt in this being's presence. He sensed that the church's interpretation and image of Christ may have given many people the wrong impression that Christ no longer speaks powerfully, lovingly, and directly to each of us.

Rudolf Steiner also warned that the church as a social and political institution is constantly in danger of losing the force of its original impulse. Instead, like other contemporary institutions, it runs the risk of exercising only a mechanical and deadening influence on our present life. The stark and empty cross adorning the church altars fails to invoke the power of the resurrection and tends to function alongside other cultural forms of materialism in a manner Rudolf Steiner described as a continuing crucifixion of Christ in the soul-spiritual world. The cross is of our own making, as is our inability to enter into a living relationship with Christ outside the near-death state. Steiner indicated that the mystery of Christ is expressed in the description of him as the great healer or Savior.

Steiner, believed, however, that Christ is not present where any person or group is trying to rule or control others, to cajole, stamp, brand, or otherwise judge and exclude them. Conversely, he is present wherever one person — whether Buddhist, Moslem, Christian, Jew, or free spirit — does something selfless and good for someone else or creates something true and beautiful in the world.[1] The occurrence of the life review in near-death experiences across many cultures also supports this view. The renewal of the human soul through a relationship with Christ is clearly more a matter of direct experience and action than of abstract discussions of theological doctrine.

Another particularly striking similarity between Steiner's and Ritchie's view of Christ and church doctrine involves the concept of reincarnation. Both of these men directly sense the teleological role of reincarnation in Christ's companionship with humanity "even until the end of the earth." Indeed, Ritchie speaks — only after the transforming experience of his life — of reincarnation as a directly sensed truth and as

---

1. See Rudolf Steiner, *The Gospel of St. John*, vol. 103 in the Collected Works, repr. (Hudson, NY: Anthroposophic Press, 1988), p. 120.

a necessary consequence of the relationship of our spiritual existence to our life on earth. Steiner speaks the same language; for example, in Jesus' writing in the sand he saw the work of the highest power, recording the woman's moral debt for her to make good in a future life so that a part of her spiritual being would not be lost.[1]

Though it may seem so to some readers, we have in no way strayed from our subject matter: we find ourselves at the core of Plato's near-death narrative we began with, in the moment when the soldier Er describes a vision of souls meeting their individual geniuses or guides for the journey into their new lives. It is remarkable that in our age we have no quarrel with Plato concerning his views on this subject. However, it is less well known that in the nineteenth century Goethe had the same conviction.[2] And now in the twentieth century, we magnanimously tolerate pronouncements about reincarnation from people such as Ramakrishna or Gandhi. However, hearing a modern Westerner speak in this vein suits us as little as seeing photographs of the masses in the Far East outfitted in modern sports attire. Of course, it is a matter of complete indifference to nature which of her laws suit us and which do not — the question remains what these laws are.

The church, even when it confines itself to scripture, protests too forcefully. Matthew 11:14 is explicit on this point: "And if you are willing to accept it, he [John the Baptist] is the Elijah who was to come. He who has ears, let him hear." Elijah was a historic personality whose life is chronicled in the Old Testament in the First and Second Book of Kings; John the Baptist was equally clearly a flesh-and-blood person in the New Testament narratives. The church's rejection of reincarnation is a historical development and a historical fact. Origen and others among the early church fathers who adhered to the teaching of reincarnation were a political minority with no impact on the structure of the orthodox doctrine that was gradually erected around the events of the New Testament.

As Rudolf Steiner emphasized often, Christ's incarnation took place at the turning point of human history and will not be repeated. For him, the

1. Ibid., pp. 120-122.
2. Rudolf Eppelsheimer, *Goethes Faust: Das Drama im Doppelreich* (Stuttgart: Verlag Freies Geistesleben, 1982), pp. 251-253 and bibliography at footnote 386.

Second Coming was an Easter promise to all people, leading in the later part of the twentieth century to experiences of the Risen Christ in the etheric world similar to the one St. Paul had on the road to Damascus.[1]

The more closely we examine George Ritchie's account of his near-death experience in the light of spiritual science, the more convinced will we become that the experience directly corroborates Steiner's vision. How closely related Ritchie's and Steiner's perceptions are and how clearly they illuminate and validate each other is evident early on in Ritchie's report, as we shall see directly. While the particular word choice of the two men may differ, their language is fundamentally the same, as the details of their descriptions of spiritual reality make clear.

The Motion of the Etheric Organization

George Ritchie reports that after the panoramic life review had ended, he and his guide journeyed in spirit to a dingy all-night café and bar, where a group of sailors was drinking beer and whiskey:

> Gradually I began to notice . . . that all of the living people we were watching were surrounded by a faint luminous glow, almost like an electrical field over the surface of their bodies. This luminosity moved as they moved, like a second skin made out of pale, scarcely visible light. . . . Then, the cocoon of light must be a property of physical bodies only. The dead . . . had lost this "second skin" as well.[2]

As mentioned above, Rudolf Steiner talks about a body finer than the physical one that organizes, sustains, and interpenetrates the physical form. As he describes it, this etheric form appears to supersensible vision as a bright, thin, peach-blossom-hued aura. Steiner further indicates that this organization permeates living things only. Clearly, Ritchie's observations are consistent with this characterization: the discarnate souls lack this aura of light, but the people on the streets and in the bar are surrounded by it.

1. Rudolf Steiner, *The Reappearance of Christ in the Etheric*, vol. 118 in the Collected Works (Spring Valley, NY: Anthroposophic Press, 1983).
2. Ritchie, pp. 59, 60.

Ritchie also mentions that he himself lacked the cocoon of light, which would have to be expected if his etheric organization had remained loosely connected with his physical body in the army hospital room while an out-of-body or astral travel experience was taking place elsewhere. The fact that he did not perceive this aura surrounding his physical body in the first moments of his near-death experience does not contradict this conclusion since he did not perceive it around anyone until he had spent a certain period of time in the out-of-body state. As Ritchie explains at several points in his report, it was as if his senses had to be acclimated to the laws of the spiritual world before he was able to notice details that had been there all along. His account of his near-death experience continues:

> Then I noticed a striking thing. A number of the men [without the halo of pale light] standing at the bar seemed unable to lift their drinks to their lips. Over and over I watched them clutch at their shot glasses, hands passing through the solid tumblers, through the heavy wooden countertop, through the very arms and bodies of the drinkers around them.
>
> I watched one young living sailor rise unsteadily from a stool, take two or three steps, and sag heavily to the floor. Two of his buddies stooped down and started dragging him away from the crush.
>
> But that was not what I was looking at. *I was staring in amazement as the bright cocoon around the unconscious sailor simply opened up. It parted at the very crown of his head and began peeling away from his head, his shoulders.* . . . Instantly . . . one of the insubstantial beings who had been standing next to him at the bar . . . vanished as he hurled himself at that opening.[1]

In a lecture he presented on August 24, 1906, Steiner gave a more complete description of the etheric body and explained the modulations it undergoes under various conditions. For example, he noted that hypnosis can be dangerous because it has the effect of loosening the etheric body. According to Steiner, the etheric body of a person under hypnosis

---

1. Ibid., p. 60.

appears like "two lobes or sacks . . . hanging out . . . on both sides of the head."[1]

Understandably, our first reaction may be to assume that Ritchie must have somehow heard of Rudolf Steiner's detailed descriptions. It may seem difficult to account for the uncanny similarity of their descriptions any other way. However, it will be immediately clear that this is very unlikely when we consider the fact that Steiner had given his lecture in German and only to only a small audience. In fact, this lecture was not printed until 1943. Aside from that, Ritchie's account reflects his Protestant background and formal education but certainly shows no traces of the terminology of Rudolf Steiner's spiritual science. In a personal letter to me, Ritchie confirmed that he had never before heard of Rudolf Steiner.[2]

At this point it will be helpful to return to Steiner's first mystery drama. The character of Capesius, who very accurately and very subtly represents the pragmatic mood of questioning so characteristic of our time, objects to Theodora's account of her vision of the etheric Christ. Capesius suggests that Theodora's vision was a product of the teaching of her spiritual teacher, Benedictus. Maria, one of the other main characters, comments as follows:

> *Were this in truth the case,*
> *we would not give it weight.*
> *The fact remains, however, after careful proof:*
> *until she came into our circle,*
> *our friend knew nothing of our leader's teaching,*
> *and none of us had heard of her before.*[3]

This passage alludes to Steiner's hopes for testing his spiritual science. On another occasion he enjoined his friends more explicitly:

> I beg of you not to accept as an article of faith whatever I have said. . . . I am sure that when you begin to reflect without preconceptions, without prejudice, but simply out of the sense of truth —

1. Rudolf Steiner, *At the Gates of Spiritual Science,* lecture of August 24, 1906.
2. Correspondence of January 14 and March 17, 1988.
3. Rudolf Steiner, *The Portal of Initiation,* pp. 37-38.

when you say "We have been told this or that, let us test the original documents and texts of religion and mythology, let us test what the sciences have to tell us, too" — you will see that what was said here is correct. Turn to everything you can find to aid you, the more the better. I am unconcerned. The more you test this spring of knowledge, the more you will find its truth borne out.[1]

Here we have an example of such a test. The two descriptions of the parting of the aureole of light at the head are especially striking, not only from a purely perceptual point of view but also in regard to their conceptual contexts. Ritchie has noted in lectures that he observed the same alteration of the light around the head of a person struck on the head with a bottle; neither he nor Steiner ever saw this happen to people under conditions of normal health. The congruence of detail here functions like the artist's signature in the corner of a painting, testifying that the work is finished and genuine.

However, as Rudolf Steiner explained, spiritual truths cannot be proven once and for all; they can only be experienced. And experiencing them depends on a long process of self-transformation, on the changes our past insights have brought about in us.[2] That is plainly true; for example, there is no syllogism to prove that cannibalism is wrong. A person either directly *sees* such a truth through his or her moral faculty or does not realize it at all.

This fact is directly relevant to the mind-body question, because we are faced with the same conundrum when we wonder where the warmth of an ideal lives in a person who accepts and acts on it. It is there, but it cannot be perceived by any instrument that would measure it or by the casual bystander who would read the numbers off an EEG printout. Similarly, we can ask where the beauty of a painting by da Vinci is, in the molecules of parchment and egg tempera or in the rods and cones of the eye? And why does one person see the beauty in the painting but another cannot find it?

---

1. Rudolf Steiner, *The Mission of Individual Folk-Souls*, vol. 121 in the Collected Works, repr. (London: Rudolf Steiner Press, 1970), p. 182.
2. Rudolf Steiner, *Awakening to Community*, vol. 257 in the Collected Works (Spring Valley, NY: Anthroposophic Press, 1974), lecture of January 30, 1923.

According to Steiner, mathematical truths do not require such a special participation and transformation of the self as aesthetic and moral imagination demand — such truths can be grasped mechanically, automatically, even passively, though, of course, considerable intelligence may be required to carry out the thinking.[1] It must be admitted that there are limits to how far science and evidence — insofar as they are reduced to weight, measure, and number — can take us. At some point it becomes necessary to recognize that the aesthetic and ethical faculties are equally facts of our experience and our cognition. This element of participation becomes more and more essential to an understanding of George Ritchie's report of his near-death experience the more closely we consider the questions it raises.

The Earthbound Dead in Purgatory

George Ritchie continues his report:

> We were moving again . . . standing on the edge of a wide, flat plain. Now, however . . . I could see no living man or woman. The plain was crowded, even jammed with hordes of ghostly discarnate beings; nowhere was there a solid, light-surrounded person to be seen. All of these thousands of people were apparently no more substantial than I myself. And they were the most frustrated, the angriest, the most completely miserable beings I had ever laid eyes on. . . . Everywhere people were locked in what looked like fights to the death, writhing, punching, gouging . . . [and yet] a blow that ought to have eliminated an opponent left him exactly as before.[2]

This description accords with Rudolf Steiner's of the state of being he calls kamaloca, or purgatory, which was also accurately described both in Vedic philosophy and in the medieval Christian worldview. According to Steiner, an apocalyptic war of all against all goes on constantly just beneath the surface of everyday consciousness. The resistance of the physical body, however, prevents this from coming to our consciousness in clearly focused images during life. In Steiner's view, it is the nature of

---

1. Ibid.
2. Ritchie, pp. 63, 64.

the astral organization, to the extent that moral impulses of the ego have not laid claim to it, to assert the instinctive, elemental animal excitement of being alive against every encroachment.[1] In pandering to their pet animosities and giving in to their desire to find scapegoats, people are already preparing a place for themselves in this after-death state without knowing it.

Ritchie and Steiner both emphasize that once the body is set aside, it is too late to set a different course; the reality of the invisible company one has kept all along becomes visible suddenly and unalterably at death.

The Nearness of the Spiritual World

George Ritchie portrays the close connection between the afterlife state and life on earth that usually remains veiled during our life on earth. As he describes it, base sentiments and actions are a flow of nourishment for spiritual beings we would shudder to see near us. As he puts it, birds of a feather flock together; in other words, due to this law of affinity, we are not alone in any room or other space but are always surrounded by beings that are nourished by the thought, feeling, and will impulses we are immersed in at any moment. Sir Alfred Ayer, the noted British philosopher, had a very similar experience in June of 1988 when his heart ceased to beat for four minutes: "It was most extraordinary," said the seventy-year-old, "my thoughts became persons."[2] Many people who have survived near-death experiences have reported similar perceptions. In Ritchie's account, the insatiable being at the bar that seemed to disappear into the loosened etheric cocoon of the unconscious sailor is such a perception.

Rudolf Steiner often mentioned that beings that are the scum of the spiritual world can eclipse our free individuality if we let them; their assault on us is made easier if we engage in immoderate use of alcohol or are not sufficiently aware of the ideals informing our life. Such spiritual "leeches" are depicted in many works of medieval art, and seeing

---

1. Rudolf Steiner, *The Effects of Spiritual Development*, vol. 145 in the Collected Works, 3d ed. (London: Rudolf Steiner Press, 1978).
2. John Ezard Ayer "Thoughts from the Other Side," *The Manchester Guardian*, September 11, 1988, p. 21.

them — for example, in the cathedral at Chartres — can be immediately fruitful even without considering the question of whether or in what sense they are real.

Whether or not we understand the writhing, grappling forms on the plain in Ritchie's report to be pictures of a symbiotic relationship with beings or mental states, we can see ourselves and the world around us in them. Once we can see them as representing our own hidden, furious attachments to barbarism and buffoonery, the wish for swift, just, and severe punishment of people who are destroying the world around us dissipates. Instead, we are permeated by the insight that the work we have to do on ourselves is more than enough to occupy us, and we begin to feel empathy with the failings of others in the light of our own.

George Ritchie arrives at the insight that "whether it was a physical appetite, an earthly concern, an absorption with self — whatever got in the way of His Light created the separation into which we stepped at death."[1] It is a matter of general experience that we tend to become possessed by the very objects we are driven to possess. For some of us it is wealth that stands between us and the serenity of freedom, for others it is pride or hate, alcohol or fear. Such possessions can drive us all our lives without our realizing it. Some of us are fortunate enough to awaken to the truth that they have been caught in waking dreams after a severe trial in life or perhaps in the moment of death; others never wake up. Nevertheless, in every moment we have the opportunity to become aware of the shape of our own illusions if we are willing to face this truth. Then the will awakens, and after we have freed ourselves of the "foreign possessions," we can be our true selves and the Christ light can shine through us.

Suicides

In his report of his near-death experience, George Ritchie then describes the agony of the souls that were futilely but ceaselessly trying to taste the alcohol in the glasses of the revelers at the bar and grill. He recounts how a young man trailed everywhere behind his father, constantly imploring him for forgiveness with soundless words and invisible

---

1. Ritchie, p. 67.

gestures. He describes seeing this scene reenacted by countless souls around him over and over again. He is baffled until his guide explains to him that he is showing him suicides, "chained to every consequence of their act."[1] This description of the pain and anguish of the soul after suicide is strikingly similar to Rudolf Steiner's. According to Steiner, from the first moment of death, suicides experience the loss of the body as immeasurable suffering and loss.[2] In contrast to those who die naturally or accidentally, people who have committed suicide have deprived themselves of the ability to carry out the tasks and harvest the experiences that were the reasons for their births, and they crave futilely to regain the instrument they need to finish out their destinies. And if the suicide is committed early in life, Steiner observes, the soul may fail in the afterlife to meet the being the Judeo-Christian tradition calls God the Father.

The word "suicide" in English is innocuous enough; the German word for it literally means "self-murder," an apt word for what Steiner and Ritchie describe. In reporting suicides, the German press avoids these uncomfortable associations by using the euphemism "death by free choice." In every country, people who kill themselves hope that there is no moral power higher than themselves to hinder them. What these two men are telling us is a pointed affront to this abstract notion of freedom. They are saying that we are responsible for our lives according to principles that go beyond what our physical senses can register and cope with.

It may be particularly galling to some people to have to realize that there are aspects of the world we can only experience through the window of moral intuitions. After all, some of us may have been taught that moral intuitions are only subjective and illusory while sensory experiences, which can be weighed, measured, and otherwise quantified, are concrete, substantial, and objective. Ritchie's account of his near-death experience and Steiner's writings both indicate that by focusing on physical reality and its quantitative aspects we are in fact arbitrarily defining the parameters of meaning in our lives. The seemingly clear distinctions in this either-or thinking and in input-output models of human behavior are only superficial. Neither these nor the social institutions built upon

---

1. Ibid., p. 59.
2. Arenson, p. 821.

them can provide an answer to the vast mystery of human life and human nature; the disdain etched in the face of the Egyptian Sphinx outlasts our abstract institutions.

Guardian Angels

Ritchie's narrative continues:

> Gradually I was becoming aware that there was something else on that plain of grappling forms. Almost from the beginning I had sensed it, but for a long time I could not locate it. [It] left me stunned.
>
> [Over the entire plain were hovering beings that were] seemingly made of light. It was their very size and blinding brightness that had prevented me at first from seeing them. Now . . . I could see that these immense beings were bending over the little creatures on the plain. . . . I realized with bewilderment that I had been seeing them all along, without ever consciously registering the fact. . . . They had been present in the streets, the factories, the homes, even in that raucous bar. And suddenly I realized . . . whether it was a physical appetite, an earthly concern, an absorption with self—whatever got in the way of His Light created the separation into which we stepped at death.[1]

Again and again we find that Ritchie has brought back, so to speak, whole stretches of Rudolf Steiner's anthroposophy from his nine-minute journey. Rudolf Steiner also talked about this image of countless guardian angels watching over the living and the dead:

> An angel watches over every human being, and the task of this being is to preserve the human astral body from total destruction in the earthly life and to lead the human soul from incarnation to incarnation. This being is the prototype of the human being, and it is the hope of the soul to become ever more like this being. . . . The guardian angel is spiritually identical to the higher self of the human being to which the latter looks up.[2]

---

1. Ritchie, p.67.

This is reminiscent of the puzzling ending to Plato's story of Er, the soldier who underwent a near-death experience, particularly of the scene where the souls of the dead draw lots to meet the guide who will lead them into their new lives.

How is the individual's guardian angel or higher self related to Christ? According to the Gospel of St. John, Christ promised that after the Ascension he would send the Comforter, the Holy Spirit he first received like an angelic dove over the water of the Jordan at the Baptism. Interestingly enough, Steiner discusses the moral-spiritual transformation of the astral body in terms of the birth of the Holy Spirit in the human soul or of the higher self within each individual.[1] Apparently, in the spiritual world these innumerable higher selves are simultaneously perceived as individual beings and as the one Holy Spirit.

Ritchie's and Steiner's understanding of guardian angels both seem to suggest that our hardships are not the empty sufferings they appear to be when we look at them as merely physical events. In the context of an invisible spiritual-moral world interwoven with physical existence, our hardships and sufferings are not a matter of indifference to these higher beings. If we can hold on to this image, the eyes of our souls will be opened to how crucial it is that we meet the tasks life sets us and to how important the fulfillment of even the painful tasks is to the invisible purpose of our lives.

Another particularly significant implication of both Ritchie's and Steiner's perceptions of the Holy Spirit as the guardian angel for every soul is that the Holy Spirit or Christ can appear to any soul during a near-death experience as a being of light, regardless of what that person's religious persuasion might be, According to Steiner, individual aspects of Christ are designated by different names in non-Christian cultures; in particular, he speaks about Krishna as the light of Christ that Paul saw on the road to Damascus.[2] However disconcerting this insight may initially

2. Rudolf Steiner, *Universe, Earth and Man*, vol. 105 in the Collected Works (London: Rudolf Steiner Press, 1987).
1. Rudolf Steiner, *The Structure of the Lord's Prayer*, (London: Rudolf Steiner Press, 1971).
2. Rudolf Steiner, *The Bhagavad Gita and the Epistles of Paul*, vol. 142 in the Collected Works (New York: Anthroposophic Press, 1971), p. 98.

seem in the context of orthodox church doctrine, it must be true if Christ is more than an invention of Western church history. It must be true if Christ lives and works for the well-being of every human soul.

Devachan, the Realm of Creative Thought

George Ritchie's narrative continues:

> We were moving again. Or rather, the scene in front of us was — changing somehow. Opening up. It was the quality of the light that was different, as though the air had suddenly become more transparent, enabling me to see what had apparently been there all along.[1]

A third world is revealed to him, as different from purgatory as that world was from the realm of the panoramic review. It is striking that Steiner used almost exactly the same form of expression to describe what he called the higher or supersensible worlds of experience, in particular the regions he referred to with the Sanskrit word *devachan* or its translation "spiritland":

> The regions of spiritland do not lie next to each other like sections. They interpenetrate each other, and the human being experiences himself in a new region not because he has externally entered upon it in any form whatever, but because he has attained in himself the inner capacities for now perceiving what he has previously lived within, but without perceiving it.[2]

As Steiner explains, while the panoramic review involves the release of the etheric organization and purgatory the release of the astral organization, devachan is the realm of the freed creativity of the individuality. More specifically, he portrays the life-review as the laying aside of the bonds that tie the etheric body to conscious earthly experience; as a result, the soul is able to think, for the first time since the moment of conception, in supersensible pictures and to meet the guardian of the threshold.

---

1. Ritchie, p. 68.
2. Steiner, *Theosophy*, p. 119.

Purgatory, in contrast, is a state of laying aside the past attachments of the astral organization to the repeated mental states and emotional patterns that forged the particular destiny of the past life — that is, the attachments to what Goethe aptly called the "elective affinities " of the soul for the events and meetings of one's life. As Steiner sees it, in consciously appreciating these dreamlike affinities, we enter into the joy and sufferings we have caused others during our lives on earth, and we begin to hear and understand the words of the hierarchies that direct the forces of destiny according to the moral creative temperament of each soul.

Devachan is the state in which the soul lays aside the focus of the past life altogether by remembering from the world between death and rebirth the essential will nature of the eternal individuality and by recognizing all past lives as gestures of this being. At this level of consciousness the sense of self lies beyond the faculties of imagination and thinking in an unspoken rapport between creative beings; the only thing in our ordinary consciousness that can be compared to this state is a momentary glimpse of the creative will manifest in the painting of an inspired artist, or of a particular action as the perfect expression of a certain person. In this state the will concerning what has been left unfinished in past lives becomes creative through the work of the highest hierarchies. It works out of a state of blessedness to the extent that something of a moral-spiritual nature is left for the soul after the fires of purgatory have taken away its earthliness, and it works in a swoon where the soul has nothing of this nature to give beyond purgatory.

Rudolf Steiner notes that his depiction is not unique and that genuine initiations are characterized by a conscious experience of these distinct realms. For example, he describes the medieval Scandinavian *Dream Song of Olaf Asteson* as such an account.[1] The poem represents each of these realms in its spiritually imaginative picture language. At the etheric gate of death there appears the guardian of the threshold as hound, serpent, and bull. A vision of kamaloca or purgatory follows in a description

---

1. Rudolf Steiner, *Der Zusammenhang des Menschen mit der elementarischen Welt*, vol. 158 in the Collected Works (Dornach, Switzerland: Rudolf Steiner Verlag, 1980), lectures of January 1, 1912 and January 7, 1913. See also chapter 3 of Bernard Lievegoed, *Man On the Threshold: The Challenge of Inner Development* (Stroud, England: Hawthorn Press, 1985).

of the sufferings of souls mechanized by greed and shame at the hands of the witch-wives of Brooksvalin and of the weighing of souls on the scales of the archangel Michael at the throne of doom. Finally, a vision of devachan's creative state of blessedness is described for the soul in which a moral-creative element remains active and fruitful beyond purgatory. It seems, then, as though Ritchie's description of three levels or realms provides an additional illustration of the principle Steiner indicates.

Paradoxically, Steiner characterizes the third realm or devachan as the one most closely related to the events and landscape of the earth and to the blessedness of creating in the material world. This connection is also illustrated in Ritchie's account of his near-death experience in his description of the beings he saw in the light of the third realm, beings that appeared to be wrapped in thought like monks in cowls and that were working on a spherical building with a catwalk at a spiritual university. At first, this picture may call to mind Swedenborg's visions of a spiritual world of cultivated lawns and houses and Rudolf Steiner's criticism that Swedenborg "insisted on acknowledging as true only what he could calculate and perceive with his senses. . . . [And] he drew the supersensible world down into a lower sphere under the influence of his habits of natural science."[1] Indeed, this criticism applies to the many accounts of near-death experiences that report flowery meadows, celestial gates and townships, and it would appear to apply to some extent also to Ritchie's narrative due to the earth-bound nature of the etheric organization and the physical body.

However, in this connection, too, George Ritchie's narrative is quite special. He reports that nine years after his experience he was amazed to see a drawing of the prototype for the first nuclear submarine in *Life* magazine and that it was precisely this construction that he had seen "cowled monks" working on in his spiritual vision. Clearly, he appears to be reporting a vision of what Steiner calls the fourth region of devachan or the realm of inventive thought. Steiner explains that "all that we develop during earthly life in the way of scientific discoveries, artistic ideas and

---

1. Rudolf Steiner, *History of Spiritism* (New York: Anthroposophic Press, 1943).

forms, technical concepts, bears fruit in this fourth region. It is out of this region, therefore, that artists, scientists, and inventors draw their impulses."[1] The salient characteristic of this fourth realm is a creative power that works not only in souls but also into the shape and will nature of the material earth itself.

It should be emphasized here that Steiner meant something very different with terms such as "fourth region" from what is usually understood by them. He pointed out that the higher regions of the spiritual world all interpenetrate each other and the material earth. The idea of space as we know it in the physical world is of no use in distinguishing "high" and "low" as they are meant in such a description. The etheric and astral organizations, purgatory, and devachan do not in any sense of the word occupy physical space or fit into mechanistic concepts. Their relative connections to the physical elements have to be thought of in terms of affinity and not width, breadth, or distance. Indeed, in regard to these realms two strangers on a bus are further apart than brothers on different continents.

In this context it is interesting to note that modern physicists are leaving the Newtonian parameters behind, as is evident in the following pronouncement Sir James Jean made in 1937: "Today there is a wide measure of agreement, which on the physical side of science approaches almost to unanimity, that the stream of knowledge is heading toward a nonmechanical reality; the universe begins to look more and more like a great thought rather than like a great machine."[2] Thinking in mechanistic terms is of little use in approaching spiritual science; its higher, living lawfulness begins to become apparent only after a period of acclimatization.

Return to Ordinary Consciousness

Contemplating the Christ-like prototypes in the realm of pure inventive thought, Ritchie found himself suddenly transported back into his body in the hospital room, but for a short time he was still in the company of his guide. In his narrative he simply reports that he was told things he cannot repeat. Here again we are confronted with one of the characteristic

---

1. Steiner, *Theosophy*, p. 121.
2. Koestler, p. 58.

elements of what Rudolf Steiner called initiation experience. In his essay entitled, *The Chymical Wedding of Christian Rosenkreutz,*[1] Steiner indicates that there is a special reference to the characteristics of a true initiation behind Andreae's report of a missing folio at the end of the book, which the author cannot replace for the reader. And so it is at the end of George Ritchie's account as well. The essence of such an initiation is spoken in the Holy of Holies or the spiritual name of an individual; it is with this name that the highest in the human being strives to unite in the course of development. Steiner describes initiation as an event that many people are familiar with, if not as profoundly as the author of the *Book of Revelation* was. He describes how enduring a particular trial of life may spiritually awaken an individual to a new sense of purpose and confidence.[2] Sabom, Ring, Moody, and others who have studied cases of near-death experiences in depth have noted that the most significant aspect of these events is the change they engender in people's lives. Kenneth Ring points out that very frequently a person who has undergone such a near-death experience afterwards tends to be more interested in life, less concerned about material things, more self-confident, independent, purposeful, more able to engage in solitary and contemplative pursuits, more ready to find delight in nature, and more tolerant and compassionate toward others.[3]

The peace St. Paul spoke of as transcending all understanding takes on life and new meaning when we meet such people. Significantly, such persons tend to have a heightened sense of the moral-spiritual element of life that is grounded in present experience and not sectarianism.[4]

Noyes and Kletti found that persons who survive life-threatening situations, whether or not they undergo physical trauma or an apocalyptic vision, also tend to acquire a sense of relative invulnerability and lose much of their fear of death; they sense a greater meaning in life and often feel especially blessed. This is clearly true for Ritchie. Perhaps the

---

1. In Paul Allen, ed., *A Christian Rosenkreutz Anthology*, 2d ed. (Blauvelt, NY: Rudolf Steiner Publications, 1974).
2. Rudolf Steiner, *Knowledge of the Higher Worlds and Its Attainment*, vol. 10 in the Collected Works (Spring Valley, NY: Anthroposophic Press, 1984), ch. 3.
3. Zaleski, p. 142.
4. See Zaleski, pp. 145-147.

outstanding moment, discussed below, in his entire account of his near-death experience is one of the most mundane; in any event, it is very impressive.

George Ritchie ultimately served in the medical corps during the war, and one of his war experiences involved an injured Air Force sergeant whom he treated in a field hospital near Rethel, France, early in 1945. The soldier was in considerable pain while Ritchie attended to him, but he wanted to exchange introductions and talk. He asked Ritchie where he was from, what kinds of things he liked to do, whether he had any brothers and sisters. Ritchie's preconception of foul-mouthed, small-minded sergeants was dissolving, and he found himself asking the sergeant about himself. The sergeant's name was Jack Helms; he was from El Dorado, Arkansas, where he had been working in a restaurant when the war began. Now, on the other side of the world, his jeep had set off a land mine. Ritchie found something about the smile of this rugged and good-natured soldier unforgettable. Despite the pain of his leg injury, he seemed more concerned about Ritchie's problems and future than his own. The sergeant seemed to take the same interest in all of the staff and soldiers.

As the sergeant recuperated, he and Ritchie occasionally took walks together, and Ritchie felt as if they had known each other before. One day, without having intended to do so, Ritchie found himself recounting for the second time the events of that winter night in Fort Barkley, Texas: about the hospital movie theater, the ward boy, the ambulance, the X-ray station, the stranger in his bed, and then the all-night café. It was clear that the sergeant had never heard anything like the things Ritchie was telling him, but it was also obvious that he was listening very intently, taking everything in. Ritchie all of a sudden realized why Jack Helms had seemed to him so familiar and so compelling a personality all along: "It was Christ who all this time had been looking at me out of Jack Helms' eyes." Five thousand miles away and several years later, on a hillside in France, George Ritchie recognized the presence of the Genius of his life for the second time.

Experiences such as Ritchie's suggest that encountering Christ is fundamentally a matter of the awakening of our morally perceptive faculty in the oceanic flow of our sensory life with all its revelations of created form, color, motion, and eventfulness — and of which not an iota will ever be lost from the whole of the universe as it is emerging in the vision of modern physics or spiritual science, not the death of a single sparrow and not the motion of a hand pouring tea, nor the smallest loving or hateful action. The experience of Ritchie and others reveals that life always tends toward the blessedness that lives in a man like Jack Helms, but a certain habitual dullness of self-absorption and distraction, of planning, fearing, craving, or hurrying seems often to prevent it.

CODA

GEORGE RITCHIE HAS convincingly described his meeting with Christ, a meeting that made the cosmic Word a living personal experience for him. For many who are familiar with the life and work of Rudolf Steiner, Ritchie's narrative testifies also to an intimate and exact familiarity with beings and events of the spiritual world, which spiritual science makes intelligible. Steiner spoke of the twentieth century as an age at the threshold of the etheric Christ; Ritchie's story provides many opportunities to recognize and enter into the meaning of this special event.

George Ritchie Today

George Ritchie was granted a new life, which he has dedicated in many ways to the Companion who stood by him during the nine minutes he had been given up for dead. Beyond the tasks of family and work, Ritchie's renewed sense of purpose in life led him to help found a youth organization to work with troubled young people and to lecture worldwide. His book is currently available in thirteen languages. Ritchie's experience reveals that our feeble theologies do little more than obscure the sublime nature of the being whose radiance encompasses the hopes of all cultures and every human soul. Read in the light of Rudolf Steiner's spiritual science, the remarkable details of Ritchie's journey bear him out.

Rudolf Steiner and the Anthroposophical Society

Rudolf Steiner also underwent a profound Christ experience, but not under near-death conditions. In chapter 26 of his autobiography he wrote that "at the turn of the century this germ of knowledge [of the essence of Christianity] opened more and more. . . . This experience culminated in my standing in the spiritual presence of the Mystery of Golgotha in a most profound and solemn festival of knowledge."[1]

If a near-death experience can lead to an encounter with Christ and cause such a transformation in the person undergoing it, a final practical question that arises out of Rudolf Steiner's Christ vision is whether there is any need for practices and ideals that lead to a rebirth experience. Steiner's own answer to the question is a consequence of his perception of the workings of reincarnation and destiny. People encounter Christ in a near-death crisis or even in other, less traumatic conditions as a result of connections they have forged in life — in a past life or in the present one — or due to grace, the need of some spiritual beings to reveal a truth to the world through such people.

According to Steiner, many people will not be fortunate enough to encounter Christ even after death or to meet another special guiding being, such as the archangel Michael or Buddha, and some will not even meet again the souls they were close to on earth because they did not develop sufficient faculties of ethical intuition and of artistic creativity on their own initiative during their life on earth. He emphasizes that ethical intuition as well as art are the instruments of the creative work of the realm of devachan, and only creative work in the service of the evolution of the earth from out of the realm of devachan leads to a state of blessedness in devachan and in life.

Three aspects of the phenomenon of near-death experiences support this emphasis on the decisive role our conduct of life on earth plays in shaping our lives after death. First, the dominant theme in near-death experiences that leads to the panorama and judgment is regret for the many precious opportunities to act on what is truly essential in life that have been passed by for the sake of material desires and self-interest. ("What have you done with your life to show to me?" asks George Ritchie's guide.) Second, a more comprehensive study reveals that in some near-death experiences this regret is so strong that it takes the form of empty nothingness, torment, and hatefulness. Third, many of the accounts of near-death experiences are replete with sensory memories of meadows, houses and gardens, and men in business suits. They raise the

1. Rudolf Steiner, *The Course of My Life*, ch. 26.

question of whether individual faculties have to be developed in life to enable us to have spiritual experiences after death. Recall Steiner's description of the astral organization's daily subjection to the images of the senses. According to Steiner, the soul so habituates its faculty of imagery to the sensory world during life that it is of little use in apprehending the spiritual world in truly sense-free pictures, which Steiner aptly calls "Imaginations," at the time of death. The astral organization, passively oriented to the senses, continues to rely on the memory images of the sensory world in translating the supersensible experiences. As Steiner concludes from this, only through cultivation of the Imaginative life can we enable the soul to live in the spiritual world.

As Steiner saw it, our shadowy intellectual thoughts and sensory experiences mechanize our lives and draw us into a materialism that distorts our afterlife experiences, or even robs us of them, if we do not penetrate them with our understanding and soul.

Steiner's writings no longer seem speculative after we read Robert Monroe's portrayal of the body-free world in his book *Far Journeys*.[1] He describes that world as a jumble of radio signals, replete with "M-Band noise," "Load-Energy Ratios," "Building Escape Velocity Energy" and "Entry-Exit maps." There is no Christ nor any of his archangels; there is no Buddha nor any benevolent being in this world at all. Instead, there are only entities that delight in putting Mr. Monroe through obstacle courses and occasionally in leaving him in some state of torment despite any entreaty or prayer he makes to them.

According to Steiner's prediction, this kind of subnature will take the place of the spiritual world for our civilization as a whole if it remains without Christ and without true art for long in the age of technology. He introduced spiritual science as a counterweight to the soul-numbing effect of modern life; it was not to be a luxury, but the answer to a positive need of our age. In fact, he predicted that the etheric vision of the Christ meant to take hold in the twentieth century could be defeated for all but the very few if humanity as a whole does not begin to cultivate spiritual imagination and insight.

---

1. Robert Monroe, *Far Journeys* (Garden City, NJ: Doubleday, 1987).

Based on their speculative intellect, some readers may object here that the distinctions presented so far lack substance and that the above discussion of our moral-imaginative faculty, spiritual renewal, rebirth in near-death experiences, and of a subnatural world proves only that under certain physiological conditions some people dream and others do not. This objection returns us to the fundamental question of all science, philosophy, and religion, the question we began with: Is the mind a product of neurophysiological processes, or are the bodily senses the instrument of consciousness? What light has our investigation of near-death experiences shed on this question? We are now perhaps able to ask and answer this question in a broader and more subtle context than we could at the start of our inquiry.

Michael Sabom's observations of autoscopic near-death experiences and Steiner's description of the etheric body are examples of what is labeled the "shadow person" theory of immortality, which describes the soul as a real but immaterial substance. Philosophers tend to dismiss this possibility out of hand as an example of lazy thinking. They consider the soul just insubstantial enough to escape detection to not have to be subjected to any empirical tests of existence and just substantial enough to still exist apart from the physical body.[1] The underlying assumption of such objections to our conclusions is not hard to uncover: a thing that exists and perceives can be seen to exist, at least under an electron microscope or some other instrument. On closer inspection this proves to be a preconceived notion; our observations do not confirm it. Interestingly, Sabom notes that in addition to theological dogma there is such a thing as scientific dogma as well, and in the final pages of his study he warns against taking the past and present assumptions of science as proven facts. He is correct; dogma and stagnation set in the moment we cease to test our assumptions. And there would appear to be a link between the ability to observe without applying preconceived ideas and the creative vision of truly inventive scientists, such as Galileo, Einstein, and Boole.

---

1. Anthony Flew's treatment of the subject in his essay "Immortality" in *The Encyclopedia of Philosophy* (New York: Macmillan, 1967), vol. IV, pp. 139-150, is typical of this.

Rudolf Steiner and the Intelligibility
of the Observations of Spiritual Science

We accepted Rudolf Steiner's invitation to test the communications of spiritual science — and what is the result? On the level of *perceptual corroboration* spiritual science is clearly not refuted, but it is also not proven. While strange and remarkable observations, such as the parting of the etheric head under conditions of intoxication or hypnosis, lead us deeper into the mystery of human existence, the corroboration of such details alone is still no proof to the physical scientist, and this is justly so. With respect to the observer, it is certainly thinkable that the common thread is the identical physiology of the brain and of patterns of perception. It is conceivable that this detail is a representation under physiologically specific conditions of the two hemispheres of the brain. Indeed, Steiner indicates as much when he describes the etheric organization as a finely detailed double of the physical head. However, this perceptual corroboration does demonstrate that our consciousness and our existence are mysteries that ask to be discovered and solved.

On a more subtle level, we began to find a realm of *conceptual agreement of contexts* that is conclusive in a very different way from perceptual corroboration. With respect to the objects observed, particular significance attaches to the kind of lawfulness in the realms both Ritchie and Steiner describe. The consistent descriptions of living persons aglow with a cocoon of light that never surrounds lifeless matter or discarnate souls is such a pattern. The description of the folded etheric head that only appears around hypnotized and stuporous but never around fully conscious persons is another. This kind of harmony between accounts of near-death experiences and the communications of spiritual science cannot be easily reduced to a question of identical structures in the physiology of the observers.

There is a third level of corroboration between the accounts treated here and Steiner's spiritual science; however, it is not simply a fact and never can be, for here active participation is required to build the substance of the corroboration. This mode of thinking cannot be carried out in the outward-oriented and casual way we use, for example, to balance our checkbooks. We know that we apply something other than analytic thinking when we grasp that a work by da Vinci is beautiful and true, or when we form the judgment that cannibalism is evil. Here what would have been corroboration in terms of "alongside" and "one-after-the-other" becomes a participation in the living flow of this moment out of the past moment; otherwise, it is nothing at all.

In the realm of speculative ideas there is thus considerable evidence that the mind is a supersensible entity. Nothing is definite, but we have good reason to believe something. In the realm of living ideals, the supersensible character of the mind is either suddenly, fully, and directly experienced, or it is not known at all. The compositions of Mozart illustrate this, and so does the moment when we suddenly appreciate, for example, the height and majesty of an oak tree so completely that this majesty is almost felt physically and is almost audible. It is the difference between rote book-learning and an inventor's suddenly new perspective.

Science is also more and more approaching this element of participation. This is not surprising where the field of inquiry is no longer confined to the mechanical forces and relationships of the more or less solid world Newton knew. Scientist nowadays enter more and more the weaving dynamics of subatomic worlds that appear more like living thought than like a great machine. A classic illustration is the uncertainty principle of Heisenberg: whether the apparent position or the velocity of an atomic particle will be observed depends on the activity of the observer. We are inextricably interwoven with every facet of the world we live in.

Rudolf Steiner referred to Newtonian thinking as a material mode of cognition and noted that its habits and prejudices limit it to an understanding of mechanical relationships or material effects of material causes. Steiner speaks of a supersensibly living world that interpenetrates this one, and we have characterized its first manifestation as the etheric world, in which we have to do with supersensible causes of material effects and which calls for a correspondingly subtler form of thinking.[1] With the former kind of thinking we can grasp only the mechanical forces of the sensory world while, according to Steiner, the second mode of thinking is needed to comprehend the mystery of life.

---

1. Rudolf Steiner, *Karmic Relationships*, vol. 1. (London: Rudolf Steiner Press, 1972), lecture of February 16, 1924.

In Steiner's view the material mode of cognition is a passive or dead thinking, in which participation is held to a minimum, but the higher, living form of thinking enters into perception and the details of perception. There is nothing all that mysterious about this distinction of modes of thinking; it is no secret that novelists, for example, tend to be particularly observant. Many artists and inventors exercise the second kind of thinking frequently in their work. It is a matter of keenly and questioningly sensing and entering into any given experience or observation.

However, what Steiner and Ritchie present remains unintelligible to the mind-set of our passive thinking. To such thinking a stone is just a stone; with this thinking we will arrive at the same mineral analysis of a Zen rock garden as we get of the excavation site for a new bank building. Just as there is not and never will be a manual to make anyone who would like to be into a Mozart, no code of laws is or will ever be able to confer on the antisocial the joy of giving. The imagination creates out of a certain empty chaos of the present moment both art and loving deeds, or such art and loving deeds will not happen; the passive habits of the past cannot bring them about. The nascent state out of which all invention and art grow is also the avenue to certainty of the moral-spiritual world.

BIBLIOGRAPHY

Allen, Paul. Ed. A *Christian Rosenkreutz Anthology*. 2nd ed. Blauvelt, NY: Rudolf Steiner Publications, 1974.

Arenson, Adolf. *Leitfaden Durch fünfzig Vortragszyklen Rudolf Steiners*. Stuttgart: Verlag Freies Geistesleben, 1985.

Ayer, John Ezard. "Thoughts from the Other Side" in *The Manchester Guardian* 11. September 1988.

Barkhoff, Martin. "Ausserkörperlichkeit und okkulter Materialismus" in *Das Goetheanum* 1985.

Basforth, Terry K. *The Near Death Experience: An Annotated Bibliography*. New York: Garland Publishing, 1990.

Blackmore, Susan. "Out of the Body?" in Robert Basil, ed., *Not Necessarily the New Age*. Buffalo: Prometheus Books, 1988.

Einstein, Albert. *The Human Side*. Princeton, New Jersey, 1970.

Eppelsheimer, Rudolf. *Goethes Faust: Das Drama im Doppelreich*. Stuttgart: Verlag Freies Geistesleben, 1982.

Flew, Anthony. "Immortality," *The Encyclopedia of Philosophy*, vol. IV. New York: Macmillan, 1967.

Goldsmith, Elisabeth E. *Ancient Pagan Symbols*. New York: G.P. Putnam, 1929.

Goethe, Johann Wolfgang von. *Scientific Studies;* edited and translated by Douglas Miller. New York: Suhrkamp, 1988.

Genova, Amy. "The Near Death Experience," *McCall's* February, 1988.

Grof, Stanislav, and Halifax, Joan. *The Human Encounter with Death*. New York: E. F. Dutton, 1977.

Hillerdal, Gunnar, and Gustaffson, Berndt. *Sie erlebten Christus*. Basel: Verlag Die Pforte, 1980.

Koestler, Arthur. *The Roots of Coincidence*. New York: Random House, 1972.

Lievegoed, Bernard. *Man On the Threshold: The Challenge of Inner Development*. Stroud England: Hawthorn Press, 1985.

Meduna, L.J. "The Effect of Carbon Dioxide upon the Functions of the Brain," *Carbon Dioxide Therapy*. Springfield, Ill.: Charles C. Thomas, 1950.

Monroe, Robert. *Far Journeys*. Garden City: Doubleday, 1987.

Moody, Raymond. *Life After Life*. Atlanta: Mockingbird, 1975.

——. *The Light Beyond*. New York: Bantam, 1988.

Morse, Melvin. *Closer to the Light*. New York: Villard, 1990.

Morse, M. et al. "Childhood Near-Death Experiences" in *American Journal of Dieases of Children* 140, 1986.

Osis, Karlis, and Haraldsson, Erlendur. *At the Hour of Death.* New York, 1977.

Penfield, Wilder. *The Mystery of the Mind.* Princeton, NJ: Princeton University Press, 1975.

Penfield, Wilder, and Rasmussen. Theodore. *The Cerebral Cortex of Man.* New York 1950.

Plato. *The Republic.* translated by Paul Shorey. London: Heinemann, 1935.

Prabhavananda, Swami, and Manchester, Frederick. *The Upanishads: Breath of the Eternal.* trans. 1948; Hollywood: Vedanta Press, 1947.

Ring, Dr. Kenneth. *Life at Death: A Scientific Investigation.* New York: Coward, McCann & Geoghegan, 1980.

Ritchie, George G. *Return From Tomorrow.* Old Tappan: Fleming Revell, 1978.

Rodin, Ernst. "The Reality of Death Experiences: A Personal Perspective," *Journal of Nervous and Mental Disease* vol. 168 (May, 1980).

Sabom, Michael B. *Recollections of Death.* New York: Simon & Schuster, 1982.

Sagan, Carl. *The Dragons of Eden.* New York: Random House, 1977.

Siegel, R.K. "Hallucinations," *Scientific American* October, 1977: 132-140.

Steiner, Rudolf.

The titles of this author appear in the order assigned in the bibliographical survey: *Rudolf Steiner: Das literarische und künstlerische Werk.* Dornach, Switzerland: Verlag der Rudolf Steiner Nachlassverwaltung, 1961.

—. Vol. 9. *Theosophy.* New York: Anthroposophic Press, 1971.

—. Vol. 10. *Knowledge of the Higher Worlds and its Attainment.* Hudson, New York: Anthroposophic Press, 1984.

—. Vol. 13. *An Outline of Occult Science.* 3rd. ed. Repr. Spring Valley, NY: Anthroposophic Press, 1989.

—. Vol. 14. *The Portal of Initation.* Repr. Blauvelt, NY: Steinerbooks, 1981.

—. Vol. 17. *The Threshold of the Spiritual World.* 3rd. ed. Repr. London: Rudolf Steiner Press, 1985.

—. Vol. 26. *Anthroposophic Leading Thoughts.* Repr. London: Rudolf Steiner Press, 1985.

—. Vol. 28. *The Course of My Life.* Hudson, New York: Anthroposophic Press, 1986.

—. Vol. 52. *Spirituelle Seelenlehre und Weltbetrachtung.* Dornach, Switzerland: Rudolf Steiner Verlag, 1972.

—. Vol. 93. *The Temple Legend.* London: Rudolf Steiner Press, 1985.

—. Vol. 95. *At the Gates of Spiritual Science.* Repr. London: Rudolf Steiner Press, 1986.

—. Vol. 101. *Occult Signs and Symbols.* Spring Valley, New York: Anthroposophic Press, 1972.

—. Vol. 103. *The Gospel of St. John.* Spring Valley: Anthroposophic Press, 1984.

—. Vol. 104. *The Apocalypse of St. John.* London: Rudolf Steiner Press, 1977.

—. Vol. 105. *Universe, Earth and Man.* London: Rudolf Steiner Press, 1987.

—. Vol. 116. *The Christ Impulse and the Development of Ego Consciousness.* Spring Valley: Anthroposophic Press, 1976.

—. Vol. 118. *The Reappearance of the Christ in the Etheric.* Spring Valley: Anthroposophic Press, 1983.

—. Vol. 121. *The Mission of Folk-Souls.* London: Rudolf Steiner Press, 1970.

—. Vol. 131. *From Jesus to Christ.* London: Rudolf Steiner Press, 1973.

—. Vol. 135. *Reincarnation and Karma.* North Vancouver: Steiner Book Centre, 1977.

—. Vol. 137. *Man in the Light of Occultism.* London: Rudolf Steiner Press, 1964.

—. Vol. 138. *Initiation, Eternity and the Passing Moment.* Spring Valley: The Anthroposophic Press, 1980.

—. From Vol. 143. *Love and Its Meaning in the World.* Repr. London: Rudolf Steiner Press, 1978.

—. Vol. 145. *The Effects of Spiritual Development.* 3d ed. London: Rudolf Steiner Press, 1978

—. Vol. 158. *Der Zusammenhang des Menschen mit der elementarischen Welt.* Dornach, Switzerland: Rudolf Steiner Verlag, 1980.

—. Vol. 159/160. *Das Geheimnis des Todes.* Dornach, Switzerland: Rudolf Steiner Verlag, 1967.

—. Vol. 178. *Individuelle Geistwesen und ihr Wirken in der Seele des Menschen.* Dornach, Switzerland: Rudolf Steiner Verlag, 1974.

—. Vol. 231. *Supersensible Man.* London: Rudolf Steiner Publishing Co., 1961.

—. Vol. 234. *Anthroposophy: An Introduction.* London: Rudolf Steiner Press, 1983.

—. Vol. 235. *Karmic Relationships,* vol. 1. London: Rudolf Steiner Press, 1972.

—. Vol. 257. *Awakening to Community.* Spring Valley: Anthroposophic Press, 1974.

—. Vol. 260. *The Christmas Conference for the Foundation of the Anthroposophical Society, 1923/24.* Hudson, NY: Anthroposophic Press, 1990.

Vishnudevananda, Vishnu. *The Complete Illustrated Book of Yoga.* New York: Simon & Schuster, 1974.

Wachsmuth, Guenther. *Die Geburt der Geisteswissenschaft.* Dornach, Switzerland: Philosophischer-Anthroposophischer Verlag am Goetheanum, 1941.

Walker, George Benjamin. *Encyclopedia of Esoteric Man.* London: Routledge & Kegan Paul, 1977.

Wetzel. Joseph, tr. *The Bridge Over the River.* Hudson, NY: Anthroposophic Press, 1974

Willis, Claudia. "A Doctor Studies Patient's Recollections of Dying," *Time Magazine* 8 Feb. 1982, p. 79.

Zaleski, Carol. *Otherworld Journeys.* New York: Oxford University Press, 1987.

64